Praise for Learn Enough Tutorials

"I have nothing but fantastic things to say about @LearnEnough courses. I am just about finished with the #javascript course. I must say, the videos are mandatory because @mhartl will play the novice and share in the joy of having something you wrote actually work!"
—Claudia Vizena

"I must say, this Learn Enough series is a masterpiece of education. Thank you for this incredible work!"
—Michael King

"I want to thank you for the amazing job you have done with the tutorials. They are likely the best tutorials I have ever read."
—Pedro Iatzky

LEARN ENOUGH
JAVASCRIPT
TO BE DANGEROUS

Learn Enough Series from Michael Hartl

Visit **informit.com/learn-enough** for a complete list of available publications.

The **Learn Enough** series teaches you the developer tools, Web technologies, and programming skills needed to launch your own applications, get a job as a programmer, and maybe even start a company of your own. Along the way, you'll learn technical sophistication, which is the ability to solve technical problems yourself. And Learn Enough always focuses on the most important parts of each subject, so you don't have to learn everything to get started—you just have to learn enough to be dangerous. The Learn Enough series includes books and video courses so you get to choose the learning style that works best for you.

LEARN ENOUGH JAVASCRIPT TO BE DANGEROUS

A Tutorial Introduction to Programming with JavaScript

Michael Hartl

♠ Addison-Wesley

Boston • Columbus • New York • San Francisco • Amsterdam • Cape Town
Dubai • London • Madrid • Milan • Munich • Paris • Montreal • Toronto • Delhi • Mexico City
São Paulo • Sydney • Hong Kong • Seoul • Singapore • Taipei • Tokyo

Cover image: Philipp Tur/Shutterstock
Figures 1.5-1.9, 4.10, 10.5, 11.2-11.4: GitHub, Inc.
Figure 2.7: Replit, Inc.
Figures 2.14, 3.1, 5.9, 6.4: Courtesy of Mike Vanier
Figures 4.4, 4.5, 4.11, 7.6, 8.5: Regex101
Figures 5.4, 10.4: Google
Figure 7.4: Courtesy of David Heinemeier Hansson
Figure 8.2: OpenJS Foundation
Figure 10.2: Amazon Web Services, Inc.
Figures 10.3, 10.6: Wikimedia Foundation, Inc.

For information about buying this title in bulk quantities, or for special sales opportunities (which may include electronic versions; custom cover designs; and content particular to your business, training goals, marketing focus, or branding interests), please contact our corporate sales department at corpsales@pearsoned.com or (800) 382-3419.

For government sales inquiries, please contact governmentsales@pearsoned.com.

For questions about sales outside the U.S., please contact intlcs@pearson.com.

Visit us on the Web: informit.com/aw

Library of Congress Control Number: 2022933200

ISBN-13: 978-0-13-784374-9
ISBN-10: 0-13-784374-7

1 2022

Contents

Preface   xiii

About the Author   xvii

Chapter 1   Hello, World!   1

1.1   Introduction to JavaScript   5

1.2   JS in a Web Browser   7

    1.2.1   Deployment   10

    1.2.2   Exercise   13

1.3   JS in a REPL   14

    1.3.1   Browser Console   14

    1.3.2   Node Prompt   19

    1.3.3   Exercise   20

1.4   JS in a File   21

    1.4.1   Exercise   22

1.5   JS in a Shell Script   22

    1.5.1   Exercise   24

Chapter 2   Strings   25

2.1   String Basics   25
        2.1.1   Exercise   27
2.2   Concatenation and Interpolation   27
        2.2.1   The Backtick Syntax   31
        2.2.2   Exercises   32
2.3   Printing   33
        2.3.1   Exercise   34
2.4   Properties, Booleans, and Control Flow   35
        2.4.1   Combining and Inverting Booleans   40
        2.4.2   Bang Bang   43
        2.4.3   Exercises   44
2.5   Methods   44
        2.5.1   Exercises   49
2.6   String Iteration   50
        2.6.1   Exercises   53

Chapter 3   Arrays   55

3.1   Splitting   55
        3.1.1   Exercises   56
3.2   Array Access   56
        3.2.1   Exercises   58
3.3   Array Slicing   58
        3.3.1   Exercises   59
3.4   More Array Methods   59
        3.4.1   Sorting and Reversing   60
        3.4.2   Pushing and Popping   61
        3.4.3   Undoing a Split   61
        3.4.4   Exercises   62
3.5   Array Iteration   62
        3.5.1   Exercises   64

Chapter 4   Other Native Objects   65

4.1   Math and Number   65
        4.1.1   More Advanced Operations   66

4.1.2   Math to String   67

4.1.3   Exercises   69

4.2   Dates   69

4.2.1   Exercises   73

4.3   Regular Expressions   73

4.3.1   Regex Methods   75

4.3.2   String Methods   77

4.3.3   Exercises   80

4.4   Plain Objects   81

4.4.1   Exercise   83

4.5   Application: Unique Words   83

4.5.1   Map   87

4.5.2   Exercises   89

Chapter 5   Functions   91

5.1   Function Definitions   91

5.1.1   Sorting Numerical Arrays   92

5.1.2   Fat Arrow   94

5.1.3   Exercise   95

5.2   Functions in a File   95

5.2.1   Exercises   103

5.3   Method Chaining   104

5.3.1   Caveat Emoji   108

5.3.2   Exercises   109

5.4   Iteration for Each   110

5.4.1   Exercises   113

Chapter 6   Functional Programming   115

6.1   Map   116

6.1.1   Exercise   122

6.2   Filter   122

6.2.1   Exercise   125

6.3   Reduce   126

6.3.1   Reduce, Example 1   126

6.3.2   Reduce, Example 2   129

6.3.3   Functional Programming and TDD   132

6.3.4   Exercises   133

Chapter 7   Objects and Prototypes   135

7.1   Defining Objects   135
       7.1.1   Exercise   139
7.2   Prototypes   139
       7.2.1   Exercise   145
7.3   Modifying Native Objects   147
       7.3.1   Exercises   152

Chapter 8   Testing and Test-Driven Development   153

8.1   Testing Setup   154
       8.1.1   Exercise   159
8.2   Initial Test Coverage   159
       8.2.1   Pending Tests   162
       8.2.2   Exercises   163
8.3   Red   164
       8.3.1   Exercises   171
8.4   Green   172
       8.4.1   Exercise   177
8.5   Refactor   177
       8.5.1   Publishing the NPM Module   184
       8.5.2   Exercises   185

Chapter 9   Events and DOM Manipulation   187

9.1   A Working Palindrome Page   187
       9.1.1   Exercise   191
9.2   Event Listeners   192
       9.2.1   Exercise   200
9.3   Dynamic HTML   202
       9.3.1   Exercise   205
9.4   Form Handling   205
       9.4.1   Exercises   210

Contents

Chapter 10   Shell Scripts with Node.js   215

10.1   Reading from Files   216

　　　10.1.1 Exercise   218

10.2   Reading from URLs   218

　　　10.2.1 Exercise   223

10.3   DOM Manipulation at the Command Line   224

　　　10.3.1 Exercises   233

Chapter 11   Full Sample App: Image Gallery   235

11.1   Prepping the Gallery   235

　　　11.1.1 Prepping the JavaScript   239

　　　11.1.2 Exercise   241

11.2   Changing the Gallery Image   242

　　　11.2.1 Exercises   246

11.3   Setting an Image as Current   250

　　　11.3.1 Exercise   252

11.4   Changing the Image Info   252

　　　11.4.1 Deploying   256

　　　11.4.2 Exercise   257

11.5   Conclusion   259

　　　11.5.1 Learning More JavaScript   260

　　　11.5.2 Learning a New Language   261

Index   263

Preface

Learn Enough JavaScript to Be Dangerous is designed to get you started writing practical and modern JavaScript programs as quickly as possible, using the latest JavaScript technologies and with a focus on the real tools used every day by software developers. JavaScript is a big language with correspondingly enormous tutorials. The good news, though, is that you don't have to learn everything to get started . . . you just have to learn enough to be *dangerous*.

Unlike most JavaScript tutorials, *Learn Enough JavaScript to Be Dangerous* treats JavaScript as a *general-purpose* programming language right from the start, so our examples won't be confined to the browser. In addition to interactive HTML websites, you'll learn how to write command-line programs and self-contained JavaScript packages as well. We'll even have a chance to explore important software development practices like version control, functional programming, and test-driven development. The result is a practical narrative introduction to JavaScript—a perfect complement both to in-browser coding tutorials and to the voluminous but hard-to-navigate JavaScript reference materials on the Web.

In addition to teaching you specific skills, *Learn Enough JavaScript to Be Dangerous* also helps you develop *technical sophistication*—the seemingly magical ability to solve practically any technical problem. Technical sophistication includes concrete skills like version control and HTML, as well as fuzzier skills like Googling the error message and knowing when to just reboot the darn thing. Throughout this book, we'll have abundant opportunities to develop technical sophistication in the context of real-world examples.

Chapter by Chapter

Chapter 1 begins at the beginning with a series of simple "hello, world" programs using several different techniques, including an "alert" in the browser and a command-line shell script using *Node.js*, a fast and widely used execution environment for JavaScript programs. We'll even deploy a (very simple) dynamic JavaScript application to the live Web.

The next three chapters cover some of the most important JavaScript data structures. Chapter 2 covers strings, Chapter 3 covers arrays, and Chapter 4 covers other native objects like numbers, dates, and regular expressions. Taken together, these chapters constitute a gentle introduction to *object-oriented programming* with JavaScript.

In Chapter 5, you'll learn the basics of *functions*, an essential subject for virtually every programming language. Chapter 6 then applies this knowledge to an elegant and powerful style of coding known as *functional programming*.

Chapter 7 shows how to make custom JavaScript objects using the example of palindromes (which read the same forward and backward). We'll start off with the simplest palindrome definition possible, and then we'll extend it significantly in Chapter 8 using a powerful programming technique known as *test-driven development*. In the process, you'll learn how to create and publish a self-contained JavaScript software package called an *NPM module*.

Chapter 9 builds on the palindrome module to make a live website for detecting palindromes. In the process, we'll learn about *events*, *DOM manipulation*, *alerts*, *prompts*, and an example of an HTML *form*.

Chapter 10 covers the much-neglected topic of *shell scripts* using JavaScript. You'll learn how to read text both from local files and from live URLs. You'll also learn how to extract information from a regular text file as if it were an HTML web page.

Chapter 11 completes the tutorial by showing you how to create a real, industrial-grade website using HTML, CSS, and JavaScript. The result is an interactive image gallery that dynamically changes images, CSS classes, and page text in response to user clicks. We'll conclude by deploying the full sample website to the live Web.

Additional Features

In addition to the main tutorial material, *Learn Enough JavaScript to Be Dangerous* includes a large number of exercises to help you test your understanding and to extend the material in the main text. The exercises include frequent hints and often include the expected answers, with community solutions available by separate subscription at www.learnenough.com.

Final Thoughts

Learn Enough JavaScript to Be Dangerous gives you a practical introduction to the fundamentals of JavaScript, both in its original niche of the web browser and as a general-purpose programming language. After learning the techniques covered in this tutorial, and especially after developing your technical sophistication, you'll know everything you need to write shell scripts, publish Node packages, and design and deploy interactive websites with JavaScript. You'll also be ready for a huge variety of other resources, including books, blog posts, and online documentation. A particularly good next step is learning how to make dynamic database-backed web applications, as covered in *Learn Enough Ruby to Be Dangerous* and the *Ruby on Rails™ Tutorial*.

Learn Enough Scholarships

Learn Enough is committed to making a technical education available to as wide a variety of people as possible. As part of this commitment, in 2016 we created the Learn Enough Scholarship program (https://www.learnenough.com/scholarship). Scholarship recipients get free or deeply discounted access to the Learn Enough All Access subscription, which includes all of the Learn Enough online book content, embedded videos, exercises, and community exercise answers.

As noted in a 2019 RailsConf Lightning Talk (https://youtu.be/AI5wmnzzBqc?t=1076), the Learn Enough Scholarship application process is incredibly simple: just fill out a confidential text area telling us a little about your situation. The scholarship criteria are generous and flexible—we understand that there are an enormous number of reasons for wanting a scholarship, from being a student, to being between jobs, to living in a country with an unfavorable exchange rate against the U.S. dollar. Chances are that, if you feel like you've got a good reason, we'll think so, too.

So far, Learn Enough has awarded more than 2,500 scholarships to aspiring developers around the country and around the world. To apply, visit the Learn Enough Scholarship page at www.learnenough.com/scholarship. Maybe the next scholarship recipient could be you!

Register your copy of *Learn Enough JavaScript to Be Dangerous* on the InformIT site for convenient access to updates and/or corrections as they become available. To start the registration process, go to informit.com/register and log in or create an account. Enter the product ISBN (9780137843749) and click Submit. Look on the Registered Products tab for an Access Bonus Content link next to this product, and follow that link to access any available bonus materials. If you would like to be notified of exclusive offers on new editions and updates, please check the box to receive email from us.

About the Author

Michael Hartl (www.michaelhartl.com) is the creator of the *Ruby on Rails*™ *Tutorial* (www.railstutorial.org), one of the leading introductions to web development, and is cofounder and principal author at Learn Enough (www.learnenough.com). Previously, he was a physics instructor at the California Institute of Technology (Caltech), where he received a Lifetime Achievement Award for Excellence in Teaching. He is a graduate of Harvard College, has a Ph.D. in Physics from Caltech, and is an alumnus of the Y Combinator entrepreneur program.

CHAPTER 1

Hello, World!

As the only language that can be executed inside web browsers, *JavaScript* is an essential part of every programmer's toolkit. *Learn Enough JavaScript to Be Dangerous* is designed to get you started writing practical and modern JavaScript programs as fast as possible, using the latest JavaScript technologies (including Node.js and ES6), with a focus on the real tools used every day by software developers.

Unlike most JavaScript tutorials, we'll be treating JavaScript as a *general-purpose* programming language right from the start, so our examples won't be confined to the browser. The result is a practical narrative introduction (https://www.learnenough.com/tutorial-writing-tutorial) to JavaScript—a perfect complement both to in-browser coding tutorials and to the voluminous but hard-to-navigate JavaScript reference material on the Web.

You won't learn everything there is to know about JavaScript—that would take thousands of pages and centuries of effort—but you will learn enough JavaScript to be *dangerous* (Figure 1.1).[1]

There are no programming prerequisites for *Learn Enough JavaScript to Be Dangerous*, although it certainly won't hurt if you've programmed before. What is important is that you've started developing your *technical sophistication* (Box 1.1), either on your own or using the preceding Learn Enough tutorials (https://www.learnenough.com/courses). These tutorials include the following, which together make a good list of prerequisites for this book:

---

1. Image courtesy of Kirk Fisher/Shutterstock.

Figure 1.1: JavaScript knowledge, like Rome, wasn't built in a day.

1. *Learn Enough Command Line to Be Dangerous* (https://www.learnenough.com /command-line)

2. *Learn Enough Text Editor to Be Dangerous* (https://www.learnenough.com/text-editor)

3. *Learn Enough Git to Be Dangerous* (https://www.learnenough.com/git)

4. *Learn Enough HTML to Be Dangerous* (https://www.learnenough.com/html)

5. *Learn Enough CSS & Layout to Be Dangerous* (https://www.learnenough.com/css-and-layout)

Box 1.1: Technical Sophistication

An essential aspect of using computers is the ability to figure things out and troubleshoot on your own, a skill we at Learn Enough (https://www.learnenough.com/) call *technical sophistication*.

Developing technical sophistication means not only following systematic tutorials like *Learn Enough Command Line to Be Dangerous*, *Learn Enough Git to Be Dangerous*, *Learn Enough HTML to Be Dangerous*, and *Learn Enough CSS & Layout to Be Dangerous*, but also knowing when it's time to break free of a structured presentation and just start Googling around for a solution.

Learn Enough JavaScript to Be Dangerous will give us ample opportunity to practice this essential technical skill.

In particular, as alluded to above, there is a wealth of JavaScript reference material on the Web, but it can be hard to use unless you already know basically what you're doing. One goal of this tutorial is to be the key that unlocks the documentation. This will include lots of pointers to my favorite JavaScript source, the Mozilla Developer Network (MDN) Web Docs (or just "MDN" for short).

Especially as the exposition gets more advanced, I'll also frequently include the exact web searches I used to figure out how to accomplish the particular task at hand. For example, how do you use JavaScript to return all elements on a page that match, say, a particular CSS class? Like this: javascript css class return all elements.

In order to learn enough JavaScript to be dangerous, we'll begin at the beginning with a series of simple "hello, world" programs using several different techniques (Chapter 1), including an introduction to *Node.js*, a fast and widely used execution environment for JavaScript programs. In line with the Learn Enough philosophy of always doing things "for real", even as early as Chapter 1 we'll deploy a (very simple) dynamic JavaScript application to the live Web.

After mastering "hello, world", we'll take a tour of some JavaScript *objects*, including strings (Chapter 2), arrays (Chapter 3), and other native objects (Chapter 4). Taken together, these chapters constitute a gentle introduction to *object-oriented programming* with JavaScript.

In Chapter 5, we'll learn the basics of *functions*, an essential subject for virtually every programming language. We'll then apply this knowledge to an elegant and powerful style of coding called *functional programming* (Chapter 6).

Having covered the basics of built-in JavaScript objects, in Chapter 7 we'll learn how to make objects of our own. In particular, we'll define an object for a *phrase*, and then develop a method for determining whether or not the phrase is a *palindrome* (the same read forward and backward).

Our initial palindrome implementation will be rather rudimentary, but we'll extend it in Chapter 8 using a powerful technique called *test-driven development* (TDD).

In the process, we'll learn more about testing generally, as well as how to create and publish a self-contained software package called an *NPM module* (and thereby join the large and growing ecosystem of software packages managed by *npm*, the Node Package Manager).

In Chapter 9, we'll apply our new NPM module to a JavaScript web application: a site for detecting palindromes. This will give us a chance to learn about *events* and *DOM manipulation*. We'll start with the simplest possible implementation, and then add several extensions of steadily increasing sophistication, including *alerts*, *prompts*, and an example of an HTML *form*.

In Chapter 10, we'll learn how to write nontrivial *shell scripts* using JavaScript, a much-neglected topic that underscores JavaScript's growing importance as a general-purpose programming language. Examples include reading from both files and URLs, with a final example showing how to manipulate a downloaded file as if it were an HTML web page.

In Chapter 11, we'll apply the techniques from Chapters 9 and 10 to a real, industrial-grade website. In particular, we'll extend the sample application from *Learn Enough CSS & Layout to Be Dangerous* to add a functional *image gallery* that dynamically changes images, CSS classes, and page text in response to user clicks. (We'll be using Git to *clone* a repository directly, so you'll be able to build and deploy the image gallery even if you haven't completed *Learn Enough CSS & Layout to Be Dangerous*.)

In most cases, typing in code examples by hand is the most effective way to learn, but sometimes copying and pasting is more practical. To make the latter more convenient, all code listings from this book are available online at the following URL:

```
https://github.com/learnenough/learn_enough_javascript_code_listings
```

Although full-blown web development with a dynamically rendered frontend and a database back end is beyond the scope of this book, by the end of *Learn Enough Java-Script to Be Dangerous* you'll have a solid foundation on which to build such skills. We'll end the tutorial with pointers to additional resources for extending your Java-Script knowledge further, as well as to further Learn Enough tutorials for full-stack web development—specifically, using *Ruby* (via *Sinatra*) and *Ruby on Rails*, for which a background in JavaScript is excellent preparation.

1.1 Introduction to JavaScript

JavaScript was originally developed by computer scientist Brendan Eich for Netscape Navigator, the first commercial web browser, under the name "LiveScript" (Box 1.2). The original use of JavaScript is still its main use—namely, "making cool things happen on web pages", typically via manipulation of the Document Object Model (DOM) introduced in *Learn Enough CSS & Layout to Be Dangerous*. In recent years, though, JavaScript's role has expanded significantly, and it is now often used as a back-end and general-purpose programming language as well.

Box 1.2: What's in a Name?

What's in a name? that which we call a rose
By any other name would smell as sweet;

—William Shakespeare, *Romeo and Juliet* 2.2.45–46

What we now call *JavaScript* was originally called "LiveScript" by its creators at Netscape, but at the time of its planned release there was an enormous amount of hype about *Java*, a language developed by Sun Microsystems. In an attempt to capitalize on this hype, Netscape changed LiveScript's name to "JavaScript"—thereby causing endless confusion for developers wondering what it has to do with Java. (The answer is: nothing.)

Later on, a standardized version of JavaScript called *ECMAScript* (pronounced ECK-muh-script) was created in an effort to improve cross-browser compatibility. Technically, what most people call "JavaScript" is more properly called "ECMAScript", with JavaScript being only ECMAScript's most common implementation, but in this tutorial we follow the common convention of using "JavaScript" to refer to the language in general. The main exception to this rule is our occasional use of contracted names like "ES6", which refers to the sixth edition of ECMAScript (a particularly large and important update, adding many useful features to the ECMAScript/JavaScript standard).

Finally, it's worth noting that the misspelling "Javascript", with a lowercase "s", is extremely common, to the point of being borderline acceptable, even in relatively formal contexts. I frankly find the "Javascript" spelling to be more appealing than the rather pedantic official version, but it is technically wrong, so in this tutorial we'll stick with "JavaScript", and be technically correct.

In order to give you the best broad-range introduction to programming with JavaScript, *Learn Enough JavaScript to Be Dangerous* uses four main methods:

1. Front-end JavaScript programs running in the user's browser
2. An interactive prompt with a Node.js Read-Evaluate-Print Loop (REPL)
3. Standalone JavaScript files (including the Node Package Manager)
4. Shell scripts (as introduced (https://www.learnenough.com/text-editor-tutorial /advanced_text_editing#sec-writing_an_executable_script) in *Learn Enough Text Editor to Be Dangerous*)

We'll begin our study of JavaScript with four variations on the time-honored theme of a "hello, world" program, a tradition that dates back to the early days of the C programming language. The main purpose of "hello, world" is to confirm that our system is correctly configured to execute a simple program that prints the string `hello, world!` (or some close variant) to the screen. By design, the program is simple, allowing us to focus on the challenge of getting the program to run in the first place.

Since the original and still most common application of JavaScript is to write programs that execute on the Web, we'll start by writing (and deploying!) a program to display a greeting in a web browser. We'll then write a series of three programs using the JavaScript execution system Node.js: first in the Node REPL, then in a JavaScript library file called `hello.js`, and finally in an executable shell script called `hello`.

Throughout what follows, I'll assume that you have access to a Unix-compatible system like macOS, Linux, or the Cloud9 IDE (https://www.learnenough.com/dev-environment-tutorial#sec-cloud_ide), as described in the free tutorial *Learn Enough Dev Environment to Be Dangerous* (https://www.learnenough.com/dev-environment). If you don't have access to such a system, it's recommended that you follow *Learn Enough Dev Environment to Be Dangerous* before proceeding. (If you use the cloud IDE, I recommend creating a development environment (https://www.learnenough.com/dev-environment-tutorial#fig-cloud9 _page_aws) called `javascript-tutorial`.)

Note for Mac users: Although it shouldn't matter in *Learn Enough JavaScript to Be Dangerous*, it is recommended that you use the Bourne-again shell (Bash) rather than the default Z shell to complete this tutorial. To switch your shell to Bash, run

chsh -s /bin/bash at the command line, enter your password, and restart your terminal program. Any resulting alert messages are safe to ignore. See the Learn Enough blog post "Using Z Shell on Macs with the Learn Enough Tutorials" (https://news.learnenough.com/macos-bash-zshell) for more information.

1.2 JS in a Web Browser

Even though JavaScript is increasingly used as a general-purpose programming language, it still thrives in its native habitat of the web browser. Accordingly, our first "hello, world" program involves displaying a notification, or *alert*, created by JavaScript code on a web page.

We'll begin by making a directory for this tutorial using **mkdir -p** (which creates intermediate directories as necessary),[2] along with an HTML index file using the **touch** command:[3]

```
$ mkdir -p ~/repos/js_tutorial
$ cd ~/repos/js_tutorial
$ touch index.html
```

Next, we'll follow the practice introduced (https://www.learnenough.com/git-tutorial/getting_started#sec-initializing_the_repo) in *Learn Enough Git to Be Dangerous* and put our project under version control with Git:

```
$ git init
$ git add -A
$ git commit -m "Initialize repository"
```

At this point, we're ready to make our first edit. We'll start in familiar territory by adding a simple HTML skeleton (without JavaScript) to our index page, as shown in Listing 1.1. The result appears in Figure 1.2.

---

2. If you're using the cloud IDE recommended in *Learn Enough Dev Environment to Be Dangerous*, I suggest replacing the home directory ~ with the directory **~/environment**, though the tutorial should work the same either way.

3. You can find coverage of Unix commands like these in *Learn Enough Command Line to Be Dangerous*.

Listing 1.1: An HTML skeleton.

index.html

```
<!DOCTYPE html>
<html>
  <head>
    <title>Learn Enough JavaScript</title>
    <meta charset="utf-8">
  </head>
  <body>
    <h1>Hello, world!</h1>
    <p>This page includes an alert written in JavaScript.</p>
  </body>
</html>
```

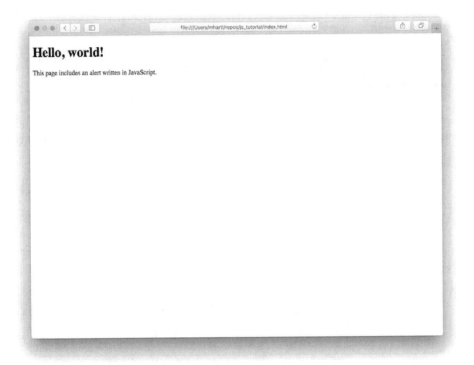

Figure 1.2: Our initial static index page.

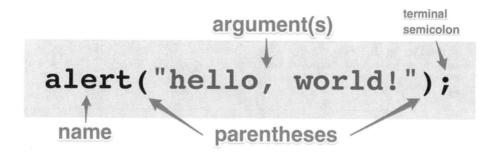

Figure 1.3: The anatomy of a JavaScript function call.

This page's paragraph is a little lie, because we haven't yet added any JavaScript. Let's change that by putting in a **script** tag containing a single command:

```
<script>
  alert("hello, world!");
</script>
```

Here we've used **alert**, which is a JavaScript *function*, a piece of code that takes in arguments and performs some task with them. As shown in Figure 1.3, the anatomy of a JavaScript function call is the function's name, an open parenthesis, zero or more arguments, a closing parenthesis, and a semicolon to end the line. (We'll learn more about functions, including how to define our own, in Chapter 5.)

In this case, **alert** takes in a *string* (Chapter 2) and displays it as an alert in the browser. To see this in action, let's add the **alert** code to our index page, as shown in Listing 1.2. Technically, we could place the **script** tag anywhere on our page, but it's conventional to place it in the **head** of the document (especially when including external JavaScript files, as we'll see in Section 5.2).

Listing 1.2: "Hello, world!" in JavaScript.
index.html

```
<!DOCTYPE html>
<html>
  <head>
    <title>Learn Enough JavaScript</title>
    <meta charset="utf-8">
    <script>
      alert("hello, world!");
```

```
    </script>
  </head>
  <body>
    <h1>Hello, world!</h1>
    <p>This page includes an alert written in JavaScript.</p>
  </body>
</html>
```

Upon refreshing the page, our browser now displays a friendly greeting (Figure 1.4).

1.2.1 Deployment

As a final step, let's deploy our incredibly fancy JavaScript app to the live Web. Our technique is the same one covered in *Learn Enough Git to Be Dangerous*, *Learn Enough*

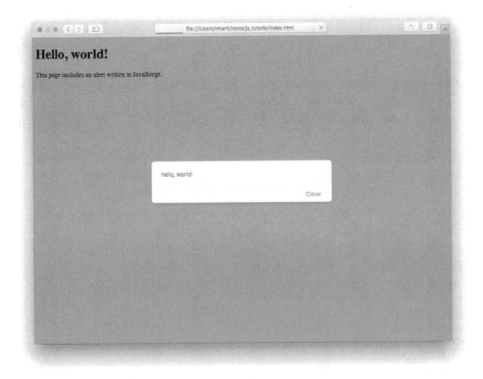

Figure 1.4: The result of a "hello, world!" alert.

HTML to Be Dangerous, and *Learn Enough CSS & Layout to Be Dangerous*, namely, a free site hosted at GitHub Pages.

Deploying at even this early stage is a powerful proof-of-concept—all kidding aside about our "incredibly fancy" app, we really are deploying a live website, which was an enormously difficult step only a few years ago, and yet now we can do it in seconds.

First, let's commit the changes made in Listing 1.2:

```
$ git commit -am "Add a JavaScript 'hello, world'"
```

The next step is to create a new remote repository at GitHub, as shown in Figure 1.5. (If any of these steps are unfamiliar, consult *Learn Enough Git to Be Dangerous* for details.)

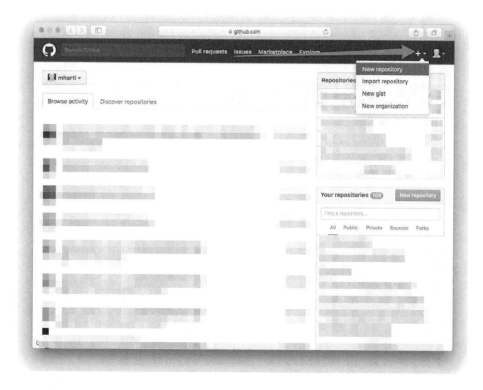

Figure 1.5: Creating a new repository at GitHub.

Next, configure your local system with the remote repository and push it up (taking care to fill in **<username>** with your GitHub username and using a GitHub personal access token when prompted for a password) and then push it up:

```
$ git remote add origin https://github.com/<username>/js_tutorial.git
$ git push -u origin main
```

Because videos are relatively hard to update, the screencasts that accompany this book use **master**, which was the default branch name for the first 15+ years of Git's existence, but the text has been updated to use **main**, which is the current preferred default. See the Learn Enough blog post "Default Git Branch Name with Learn Enough and the Rails Tutorial" (https://news.learnenough.com/default-git-branch-name-with-learn-enough-and-the-rails-tutorial) for more information.

To complete the deployment, all we need to do is edit the Settings (Figure 1.6) and configure our site to be served off the **main** branch by GitHub Pages, as shown in Figures 1.7 and 1.8.

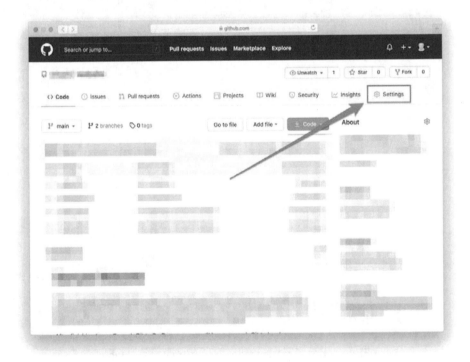

Figure 1.6: Editing the settings for a GitHub repository.

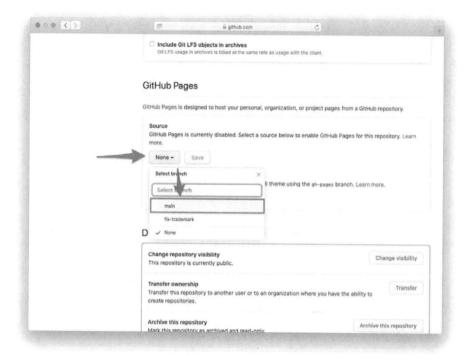

Figure 1.7: Serving our website from the `main` branch.

With that, you can now visit your site at the following URL:[4]

```
https://<username>.github.io/js_tutorial
```

The result should be the same "hello, world!" greeting seen in Figure 1.4, except now on the live Web (Figure 1.9). "It's alive!" (Figure 1.10).[5]

1.2.2 Exercise

1. What happens if you put a second alert after the first one?

---

4. To learn how to host a GitHub Pages site using a custom domain, see the free tutorial *Learn Enough Custom Domains to Be Dangerous* (https://www.learnenough.com/custom-domains).

5. Image courtesy of Niday Picture Library/Alamy Stock Photo.

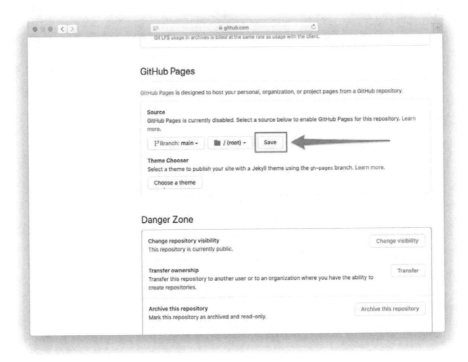

Figure 1.8: Saving the new GitHub Pages settings.

1.3 JS in a REPL

Our next two closely related examples of a "hello, world" program involve a Read-Eval-Print Loop, or *REPL* (pronounced "repple"). A REPL is a program that **read**s input, **eval**uates it, **print**s out the result (if any), and then **loop**s back to the read step. Most modern programming languages provide a REPL, and JavaScript is no exception. In fact, as hinted above, it actually provides two.

1.3.1 Browser Console

Our first example of a REPL is the browser *console*, which is available in most modern browsers as part of the standard suite of developer tools. Whether these tools are available by default depends on the browser you use; they're included automatically

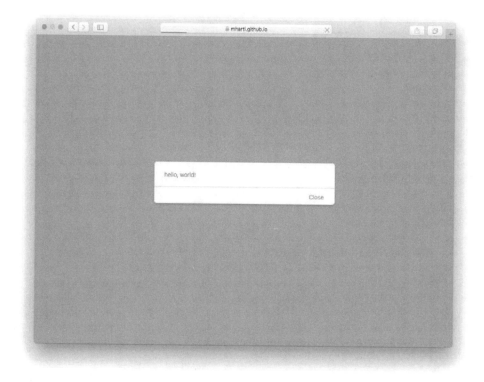

Figure 1.9: A JavaScript "hello, world!" page on the live Web.

Figure 1.10: Bringing a site to life is easier than it used to be.

Figure 1.11: Activating the developer tools via Inspect Element.

in Google Chrome, for example, but in Safari they have to be installed. Use your technical sophistication (Box 1.1) to figure out the setup for your browser of choice.

The developer tools can typically be accessed by right-clicking (or Ctrl-clicking) in your browser window and selecting Inspect Element to open the web inspector (Figure 1.11). The result should look something like Figure 1.12.

At this point, we're ready to access the console by clicking on the corresponding tab in the developer tools, as shown in Figure 1.13. As we'll see in Section 5.2, the console is a valuable debugging tool, as it has access to the full DOM and other aspects of our application's environment, as well as displaying any warnings or errors that might affect our application. In particular, note that Figure 1.13 shows a warning

Figure 1.12: The browser developer tools.

(regarding a missing **favicon.ico** file); knowing when you can and can't safely ignore such warnings is a hallmark of technical sophistication. (In this case, it's safe to ignore. In addition, your setup may or may not show the exact same error. Is that a problem?)

We're finally ready to write our "hello, world" program using the console REPL. Our method is to use **console**, which is a JavaScript *object* that represents the console and its associated data, functions, etc. In particular, the **console** object has a function called **log**, which prints out ("logs") its argument to the screen. We can access it using a "dot" notation that has become standard across a wide variety of *object-oriented* languages, as seen in Listing 1.3.

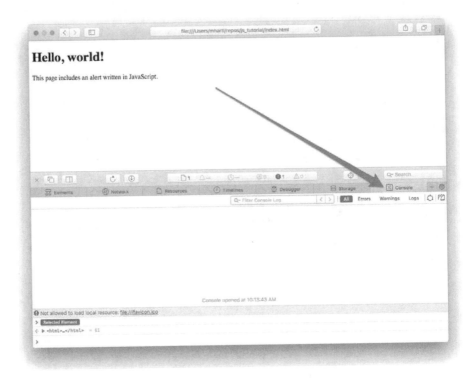

Figure 1.13: The interactive JavaScript console.

Listing 1.3: A "hello, world" command in the console.

```
> console.log("hello, world!");
```

In the context of objects, a function like **log** called using the dot notation is often called a *method*.

At this point, you should type the **console.log** command into your browser console, noting that the **>** in Listing 1.3 represents the console prompt itself, and shouldn't be typed literally. The result should resemble Figure 1.14. (We'll explain the meaning of **undefined** in Section 2.3.)

Alert readers (no pun intended) might have noticed that the command in Listing 1.3 includes a terminating semicolon (Figure 1.3), whereas the command shown in Figure 1.14 doesn't. This discrepancy is included in order to show that

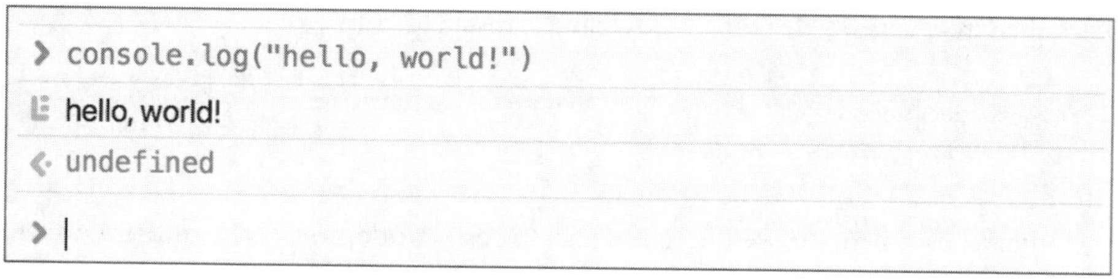

```
> console.log("hello, world!")
  hello, world!
< undefined
> |
```

Figure 1.14: Printing out "hello, world!" in the browser console.

the two commands work the same, and it is common to omit the semicolon when using an interactive console. For consistency, we'll generally include the semicolon throughout the rest of this tutorial (even in consoles), but it's good to be aware of both conventions in case you see something different in other people's code.

1.3.2 Node Prompt

Every web browser in the known Universe can execute JavaScript programs, but part of treating JavaScript as a general-purpose programming language means running it at the command line as well. This means installing and using a command-line program capable of evaluating JavaScript programs, and nowadays the most popular choice is abundantly clear: Node.js (usually pronounced "node jay-ess", and often called "Node" for short).

It's possible that Node.js is already installed on your system. The easiest way to check is to use the **which** command (as described (https://www.learnenough.com /command-line-tutorial/inspecting_files#sec-downloading_a_file) in *Learn Enough Command Line to Be Dangerous*):

```
$ which node
/usr/local/bin/node
```

If the path to a **node** executable is displayed, you're good to go.

If Node isn't present on your system, you should install it at this point. If you're using a Macintosh with Homebrew (https://www.learnenough.com/dev-environment-tutorial#sec-homebrew) installed, you can run

```
$ brew install node
```

to get the latest version. If you already have it installed, run

```
$ brew upgrade node
```

instead.

Otherwise, go to the Node.js website (https://nodejs.org/en/) and follow the download and installation instructions for your system.

Once it's installed, running the Node.js REPL is easy—just run the **node** command at the command line, as seen in Listing 1.4.

Listing 1.4: Bringing up the Node prompt at the command line.

```
$ node
>
```

As with the browser console, **>** represents the Node prompt, and like the console it allows us to run commands interactively. (For simplicity, we'll sometimes use "console" to refer either to the browser console or to the Node REPL.) In particular, to replicate the "hello, world" program from Listing 1.3, we can simply type the same command at the Node prompt, as follows:

```
> console.log("hello, world!");
hello, world!
```

(Depending on your system, you might see **undefined** appear as well; we'll discuss this detail in Section 2.3.)

That's it! In both the browser console and Node prompt, we can print "hello, world!" with this single command:

```
> console.log("hello, world!");
```

1.3.3 Exercise

1. What happens if you run an **alert** in the browser console? What about in the Node console?

1.4   JS in a File

As convenient as it is to be able to explore JavaScript interactively, most Real Pro-gramming™ takes place in text files created with a text editor. In this section, we'll show how to create and execute a JavaScript file with the same "hello, world" program we've discussed in the previous two sections. The result will be a simplified prototype of the reusable JavaScript files we'll start learning about in Section 5.2.

We'll start by creating a JavaScript file (with a **.js** file extension) for our **hello** program:

```
$ touch hello.js
```

Next, using our favorite text editor, we'll fill the file with the contents shown in Listing 1.5. Note that the code is exactly the same as in Listing 1.3 and subse-quent examples, with the difference being that in a JavaScript file there's no command prompt **>**.

Listing 1.5: A "hello, world" program in a JavaScript file.
hello.js

```
console.log("hello, world!");
```

At this point, we're ready to execute our program using the same **node** command we used in Listing 1.4 to bring up the Node prompt. The only difference is that this time we include an argument with the name of our file:

```
$ node hello.js
hello, world!
```

As before, the result is to print "hello, world!", this time to the terminal screen. (Inside the program, the return value of **console.log** is **undefined** as before, but it's not displayed since, unlike with interactive prompts, return values aren't displayed by command-line programs.)

Although this example is simple, it's a huge step forward, as we're now in the position to write JavaScript programs much longer than could comfortably fit in an interactive console or Node session.

1.4.1 Exercise

1. What happens if you give **console.log** two arguments, as in Listing 1.6?

Listing 1.6: Using two arguments.
hello.js

```
console.log("hello, world!", "how's it going?");
```

1.5 JS in a Shell Script

Although the code in Section 1.4 is perfectly functional, when writing a program to be executed in the command line shell (https://www.learnenough.com/command-line-tutorial/basics#sec-man_pages) it's often better to use an *executable script* of the sort discussed in *Learn Enough Text Editor to Be Dangerous*. Now that JavaScript can be used so effectively outside the browser, it has joined more traditional "scripting languages" like Perl, Python, and Ruby as an excellent choice for writing such shell scripts.

Let's see how to make an executable script using Node. We'll start by creating a file called **hello**:

```
$ touch hello
```

Note that we *didn't* include the **.js** extension—this is because the filename itself is the user interface, and there's no reason to expose the implementation language to the user. Indeed, there's a reason not to: By using the name **hello**, we give ourselves the option to rewrite our script in a different language down the line, without changing the command our program's users have to type. (Not that it matters in this simple case, but the principle should be clear. We'll see a more realistic example in Section 10.3.)

There are two steps to writing a working script. The first is to use the same command we've seen before (Listing 1.5), preceded by a "shebang" line telling our system to use **node** to execute the script.

The exact shebang line is system-dependent; you can find the proper executable path for your system by running the **which** command:

```
$ which node
/usr/local/bin/node
```

Using this command for the shebang line in the **hello** file gives the shell script shown in Listing 1.7.

Listing 1.7: A "hello, world" shell script.
hello

```
#!/usr/local/bin/node

console.log("hello, world!");
```

We could execute this file directly using the **node** command as in Section 1.4, but a true shell script should be executable without the use of an auxiliary program. (That's what the shebang line is for.) Instead, we'll follow the second of the two steps mentioned above and make the file itself executable using the **chmod** ("change mode") command combined with **+x** ("plus executable"):

```
$ chmod +x hello
```

At this point, the file should be executable, and we can execute it by preceding the command with **./**, which tells our system to look in the current directory (dot = **.**) for the executable file. (Putting the **hello** script on the PATH (https://www.learnenough .com/text-editor-tutorial/advanced_text_editing#code
-export_path), so that it can be called from any directory, is left as an exercise.) The result looks like this:

```
$ ./hello
hello, world!
```

Success! We've now written a working JavaScript shell script suitable for extension and elaboration. As mentioned briefly above, we'll see an example of a real-life utility script in Section 10.3.

Throughout the rest of this tutorial, we'll mainly use the Node REPL for initial investigations, but the eventual goal will almost always be to create a file (either pure code or HTML) containing JavaScript.

1.5.1 Exercise

1. By moving the file or changing your system's configuration, add the **hello** script to your environment's PATH. (You may find the steps in *Learn Enough Text Editor to Be Dangerous* helpful.) Confirm that you can run **hello** without prepending **./** to the command name.

CHAPTER 2
Strings

Strings are probably the most important data structure on the Web, since web pages ultimately consist of strings of characters sent from the server to the browser, and many other kinds of programs also require string manipulation. As a result, strings make an excellent place to start our JavaScript programming journey.

2.1 String Basics

Strings are made up of sequences of characters in a particular order. We've already seen several examples in the context of our "hello, world" programs in Chapter 1. Let's see what happens if we type a string by itself (without **console.log**) into a Node session:

```
$ node
> "hello, world!"
'hello, world!'
```

A sequence of characters typed literally is called a *string literal*, which we've created here using the double quote character **"**. The REPL prints the result of evaluating the line, which in the case of a string literal is just the string itself.

There's one detail you might have noticed above: We entered the string using double quotes, but the REPL returned it using single quotes. This detail is system-dependent (for example, the console in browsers like Chrome and Safari uses double quotes for string return values), so you shouldn't be concerned if your system differs. But this small discrepancy gives us an opportunity to learn about the difference between single and double quotes in JavaScript.

Unlike many other languages, JavaScript uses double and single quotes interchangeably for almost all practical purposes. The main exception is that apostrophes have to be *escaped out* with a backslash when included inside single-quoted strings:

```
> "It's not easy being green"
'It\'s not easy being green'
```

Here the output includes a backslash in front of the apostrophe in "It's". If we were to type the same string without escaping the apostrophe, the REPL would think that the string ended after "It", leading to a syntax error:

```
> 'It\'s not easy being green'
'It\'s not easy being green'
> 'It's not easy being green'

    ^
SyntaxError: Unexpected identifier
```

What's happening here is that JavaScript sees a bare letter **s** after the string **'It'**. Since there's no identifier called **s**, the REPL raises an error (Figure 2.1).[1] (We'll have more to say about identifiers in Section 2.2 (Box 2.2).)

Similarly, inside double-quoted strings, literal double quotes have to be escaped out:

```
> "Let's write a \"hello, world\" program!"
'Let\'s write a "hello, world" program!'
```

As you might have guessed, the return value shows how no escaping of double quotes is necessary inside a single-quoted string.

A particularly important string is one with no content, consisting simply of two quotes. This is known as an *empty string* (or sometimes *the* empty string):

```
> ""
''
```

We'll have more to say about the empty string in Section 2.4.2 and Section 3.1.

---

1. Image courtesy of LorraineHudgins/Shutterstock.

Figure 2.1: Sometimes it's not easy dealing with syntax errors.

2.1.1   Exercise

1. JavaScript supports common special characters such as tabs (**\t**) and newlines (**\n**). Show that both of these special characters work with both single- and double-quoted strings. What are their effects?

2.2   Concatenation and Interpolation

Two of the most important string operations are *concatenation* (joining strings together) and *interpolation* (putting variable content into strings).

Whether we use single- or double-quoted strings, we can concatenate (join) them with the **+** operator:[2]

---

2. This use of **+** for string concatenation is common in programming languages, but in one respect it's an unfortunate choice, because addition is the canonical commutative operation in mathematics: $a + b = b + a$. (In contrast, multiplication is in some cases non-commutative; for example, when multiplying matrices it's often the case that $AB \neq BA$.) In the case of string concatenation, though, **+** is most definitely *not* a commutative operation, since, e.g., **"foo" + "bar"** is **"foobar"**, whereas **"bar" + "foo"** is **"barfoo"**. Partially for this reason, some languages (such as PHP) use a different symbol for concatenation, such as a dot **.** (yielding **"foo" . "bar"**).

```
$ node
> "foo" + "bar";     // String concatenation
'foobar'
```

Here the result of evaluating **"foo"** plus **"bar"** is the string **"foobar"**. (The meaning of the odd names "foo" and "bar" is discussed (https://www.learnenough.com
/command-line-tutorial/manipulating_files#aside-foo_bar) in *Learn Enough Command Line to Be Dangerous* (https://www.learnenough.com/command-line).) Note
also that the concatenation example includes a descriptive JavaScript *comment*
(Box 2.1), which you wouldn't ordinarily include in a REPL session, but will
sometimes be added in this tutorial for clarity.

Box 2.1: A Comment About Comments

JavaScript *comments* start with two slash characters // and extend to the end of
the line. Comments are ignored when JavaScript is executed, but they are useful
for human readers (including, often, the original author!). In the code

```
// Prints a greeting to the console.
console.log("hello, world!");  // The command itself
```

the first line is a comment indicating the purpose of the subsequent line, whereas
the second line contains both some code and a comment describing the purpose
of the line.

Sometimes you'll want to add comments to several lines at a time (which
is particularly useful for "commenting out" multiple lines of code when debugging (Box 5.1)). Any good text editor (https://www.learnenough.com/text-editor)
will allow you to select multiple lines and comment or uncomment them all
simultaneously, yielding things like this:

```
// console.log("foobar");
// console.log("racecar");
// console.log("Racecar");
```

The details vary from editor to editor, so use your technical sophistication (Box 1.1)
to figure out the command for your editor of choice.

JavaScript also supports multiline comments enclosed in /* ... */, like this:

```
/* console.log("foobar");
console.log("racecar");
console.log("Racecar"); */
```

Because of the ease with which modern text editors can apply single-line comments to multiple lines, in practice I find that I rarely use the /* ... */ syntax.

You wouldn't ordinarily include comments in console sessions, but for instructional purposes I'll sometimes include comments in what follows, like this:

```
$ node
> 17 + 42   // Integer addition
59
```

If you follow along by typing or copying-and-pasting commands into your own console, you can omit the comments if you like; the console will ignore them in any case.

Let's take another look at string concatenation in the context of *variables*, which you can think of as named boxes that contain some value (as mentioned in *Learn Enough CSS & Layout to Be Dangerous* (https://www.learnenough.com/css-and-layout) and discussed further in Box 2.2).

Box 2.2: Variables and Identifiers

If you've never programmed a computer before, you may be unfamiliar with the term *variable*, which is an essential idea in computer science. You can think of a variable as a named box that can hold different (or "variable") content.

As a concrete analogy, consider the labeled boxes that many elementary schools provide for students to store clothing, books, backpacks, etc. (Figure 2.2[3]). The variable is the location of the box, the label for the box is the variable name (also called an *identifier*), and the content of the box is the variable value.

In practice, these different definitions are frequently conflated, and "variable" is often used for any of the three concepts (location, label, or value).

We can create variables for a first name and a last name using the JavaScript command **let**, as shown in Listing 2.1.

Listing 2.1: Using **let** to assign variables.

```
> let firstName = "Michael";
> let lastName  = "Hartl";
```

---

3. Image courtesy of Africa Studio/Shutterstock.

Figure 2.2: A concrete analogue of computer variables.

Here **let** associates the identifier **firstName** with the string **"Michael"** and the identifier **lastName** with the string **"Hartl"**.

The identifiers **firstName** and **lastName** in Listing 2.1 are written in so-called CamelCase (named for the resemblance of the capital letters to humps of a camel (Figure 2.3)),[4] which is a common naming convention for JavaScript variables. Variable names conventionally start with a lowercase character, whereas *object prototypes* like **String** (Chapter 7) start with a capital letter.

Having defined the variable names in Listing 2.1, we can use them to concatenate the first and last names, while also inserting a space in between (Listing 2.2).

Listing 2.2: Concatenating string variables (and a string literal).

```
> firstName + " " + lastName;
'Michael Hartl'
```

---

4. Image courtesy of Utsav Academy and Art Studio. Pearson India Education Services Pvt. Ltd.

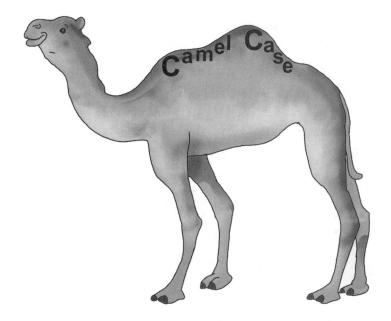

Figure 2.3: The origin of CamelCase.

By the way, the use of **let** in Listing 2.1 is characteristic of modern JavaScript (often referred to as ES6 because of the significant upgrade represented by version 6 of the ECMAScript standard (Box 1.2)). In this book, we'll always use **let** (or the closely related **const**, which we'll first see in Section 4.2) for variable assignment, but you should be aware that the use of the nearly equivalent **var** is still *extremely* common (Listing 2.3), so it's important to understand both.

Listing 2.3: Using the slightly outdated **var** to assign variables.

```
var firstName = "Michael";
var lastName  = "Hartl";
```

(You shouldn't type in Listing 2.3; it's shown only for purposes of illustration.)

2.2.1   The Backtick Syntax

Another way to build up strings is via *interpolation* using a special ES6 backtick syntax known as *template literals*:

```
> `${firstName} is my first name.`
'Michael is my first name.'
```

Here we have a string enclosed in backticks `'...'`, with the variable to be interpolated introduced with a dollar sign `$` and enclosed in curly braces `{...}`. JavaScript automatically inserts, or *interpolates*, the value of the variable `firstName` into the string at the appropriate place.[5]

We can use the backtick syntax to replicate the result of Listing 2.2, as shown in Listing 2.4.

Listing 2.4: Concatenation review, then interpolating with backticks.

```
> firstName + " " + lastName;       // Concatenation, with a space in between
'Michael Hartl'
> `${firstName} ${lastName}`;       // The equivalent interpolation
'Michael Hartl'
```

The two expressions shown in Listing 2.4 are equivalent, but I generally prefer the interpolated version because having to add the single space `" "` in between strings feels a bit awkward.

2.2.2 Exercises

1. What happens if you use **let** a second time with the same variable name? What if you use **var** instead?

2. Assign variables **city** and **state** to your current city and state of residence. (If residing outside the U.S., substitute appropriate analogues.) Using interpolation, print a string consisting of the city and state separated by a comma and a space, as in "Los Angeles, CA".

3. Repeat the previous exercise but with the city and state separated by a tab character.

---

5. Programmers familiar with Perl or PHP should compare this to the automatic interpolation of dollar sign variables in expressions like `"Michael $lastName"`.

2.3 Printing

As we saw in Section 1.3 and subsequent sections, the JavaScript way to print a string to the screen is to use the **console.log** function:

```
> console.log("hello, world!");      // Print output
hello, world!
```

This function operates as a *side effect*, which refers to anything a function does other than returning a value. In particular, the expression

```
console.log("hello, world!");
```

prints the string to the screen and then returns nothing. This is why some consoles display **undefined** after the printed value (Figure 2.4). We'll generally omit **undefined** when showing results in the REPL, but it's good to distinguish between functions that return values (almost all of them) and those like **console.log** that operate using side effects.

In contrast to many other languages—whose print functions are things like **print**, **printf** ("print format"), and **puts** ("put string")—the print function in JavaScript is rather long and cumbersome, requiring calling a method on the **console** object and using the rather unintuitive name **log**. This is due to the origins of JavaScript as a language designed specifically to run inside web browsers, rather than being designed as a general-purpose programming language.

The name **console.log** is a hint of its original purpose: to write a log to the browser console—a task at which it still excels, and which is useful in debugging. For example, we can write to the index page's console log by adding a line inside the **script** tag, as shown in Listing 2.5.

```
> console.log("hello, world!");
hello, world!
undefined
```

Figure 2.4: An undefined return value in Node.

Listing 2.5: Writing to the console log.
index.html

```
<!DOCTYPE html>
<html>
  <head>
    <title>Learn Enough JavaScript</title>
    <meta charset="utf-8">
    <script>
      alert("hello, world!");
      console.log("This page contains a friendly greeting.");
    </script>
  </head>
  <body>
    <h1>Hello, world!</h1>
    <p>This page includes an alert written in JavaScript.</p>
  </body>
</html>
```

The result is that the index page (after displaying the alert) logs the message to the console, as shown in Figure 2.5.

Finally, it's worth noting that (as seen briefly in Section 1.4.1) the default behavior for **console.log** is to insert a space:

```
> console.log(firstName, lastName);
Michael Hartl
```

This does you little good if you actually want a string representing the combination (as in Section 2.2), but it does mean you can omit the concatenation or interpolation if all you're interested in is the output.

2.3.1 Exercise

1. Define **firstName** and **lastName** variables (as in Section 2.2) inside **index.html**, and output them in the browser console using **console.log**.

Figure 2.5: The console log message on the index page.

2.4 Properties, Booleans, and Control Flow

Almost everything in JavaScript, including strings, is an object. This means that we can get useful information about strings and do useful things with them using the dot notation introduced in Section 1.3.1.

We'll start by accessing a string *property* (also called an *attribute*), which is a piece of data attached to an object. In particular, in the console we can use the **length** property to find the number of characters in a string:

```
$ node
> "badger".length;     // Accessing the "length" property of a string
6
> "".length            // The empty string has zero length.
0
```

As it happens, **length** is the *only* property of string objects, as you can verify using the MDN entry on String (https://developer.mozilla.org/en-US/docs/Web/JavaScript /Reference/Global_Objects/String) and using your browser's "Find" capability to search for the string "properties".

The **length** property is especially useful in comparisons, such as checking the length of a string to see how it compares to a particular value (note that the REPL supports "up arrow" to retrieve previous lines, just like the command-line terminal):

```
> "badger".length > 3;
true
> "badger".length > 6;
false
> "badger".length >= 6;
true
> "badger".length < 10;
true
> "badger".length == 6;
true
```

The last line uses the equality comparison operator ==, which JavaScript shares with many other languages, but there's a huge gotcha:

```
> "1" == 1;      // Uh, oh!
true
```

In other words, JavaScript considers the string **"1"** to be equal to the number **1**, at least when using == to do the comparison.

As programming languages go, this behavior is unusual, so it can be a source of frustrating bugs for people coming to JavaScript from other languages. In order to avoid confusion, it's best to use *triple equals* instead:

```
> "1" === 1;     // This is probably what you want.
false
```

Throughout the rest of this tutorial, we'll always do equality comparisons with ===.

The return values in the comparisons above, which are always either **true** or **false**, are known as *boolean* values, after mathematician and logician George Boole (Figure 2.6).[6]

---

6. Image courtesy of Yogi Black/Alamy Stock Photo.

Figure 2.6: True or false? This is a picture of George Boole.

Boolean values are especially useful for *control flow*, which lets us take actions based on the result of a comparison (Listing 2.6).

Listing 2.6: Control flow with `if`.

```
> let password = "foo";
> if (password.length < 6) {
    "Password is too short.";
  }
'Password is too short.'
```

Note in Listing 2.6 that the comparison after **if** is in parentheses, and the string is inside curly braces **{...}**.[7] We also followed a consistent indentation convention,

---

7. Such curly braces are characteristic of C-like languages, that is, languages with syntax similar to that of the C programming language.

which is irrelevant to JavaScript but is important for human readers of the code (Box 2.3).

Box 2.3: Code Formatting

The code samples in this tutorial, including those in the REPL, are designed to show how to format JavaScript in a way that maximizes readability and code comprehension. The programs executing JavaScript, whether Node or the browser itself, don't care about these aspects of the code, but human developers do.

While exact styles differ, here are some general guidelines for good code formatting:

- *Indent code to indicate block structure.* Pretty much every time you see an opening curly brace {, you'll end up indenting the subsequent line. (Some text editors even do this automatically.)

- *Use two spaces (typically via* emulated tabs *(https://www.learnenough.com/text-editor-tutorial/advanced_text_editing#sec-indenting_and_dedenting))* for indentation. Many developers use four or even eight spaces, but I find that two spaces are enough to indicate block structure visually while conserving scarce horizontal space.

- *Add newlines to indicate logical structure.* One thing I particularly like to do is add an extra newline after a series of `let` and `const` declarations, in order to give a visual indication that the setup is done and the real coding can begin. An example appears in Listing 4.6.

- *Limit lines to 80 characters (also called "columns").* This is an old constraint, one that dates back to the early days of 80-character-width terminals. Many modern developers routinely violate this constraint, considering it outdated, but in my experience the 80-character limit is a good source of discipline, and will save your neck when using command-line programs like `less` (or when using your code in a document with more stringent width requirements, such as a book (https://www.learnenough.com/courses#)). A line that breaks 80 characters is a hint that you should introduce a new variable name, break an operation into multiple steps, etc., to make the code clearer for anyone reading it.

We'll see several examples of more advanced code-formatting conventions as we proceed throughout the rest of this tutorial.

To reinforce good code-formatting practices, I'll generally format code in the Node REPL the same way I would in a file, but it's important to note that this is not

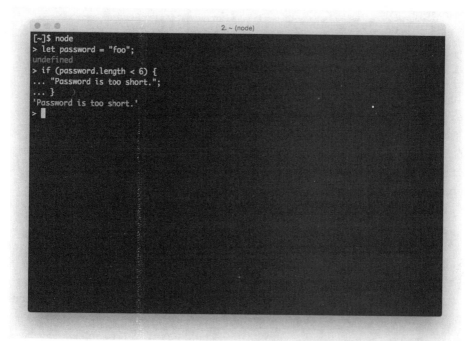

```
2. ~ (node)
[~]$ node
> let password = "foo";
undefined
> if (password.length < 6) {
... "Password is too short.";
... }
'Password is too short.'
>
```

Figure 2.7: The appearance of code in the REPL doesn't necessarily follow indentation conventions.

necessarily what you will see in the actual REPL. For example, many implementations of the Node REPL automatically insert triple dots . . . after an opening curly brace (Figure 2.7) to indicate a new block of code. This difference is not cause for concern, and you should use your technical sophistication (Box 1.1) to resolve the discrepancy between the REPL code samples and the exact appearance on your system.

We can add a second behavior using **else**, which serves as the default result if the first comparison is **false** (Listing 2.7).

Listing 2.7: Control flow with `if` and `else`.

```
> password = "foobar";
> if (password.length < 6) {
    "Password is too short.";
```

```
  } else {
    "Password is long enough.";
  }
'Password is long enough.'
```

The first line in Listing 2.7 *redefines* **password** by assigning it a new value (with no **let** required since it was already defined before). After reassignment, the **password** variable has length 6, so **password.length < 6** is **false**. As a result, the **if** part of the statement (known as the **if** *branch*) doesn't get evaluated; instead, JavaScript evaluates the **else** branch, resulting in a message indicating that the password is long enough.

2.4.1 Combining and Inverting Booleans

Booleans can be combined or inverted using the **&&** ("and"), **||** ("or"), and **!** ("bang" or "not") operators.

Let's start with **&&**. When comparing two booleans with **&&**, *both* have to be **true** for the combination to be **true**. For example, if I said I wanted both french fries *and* a baked potato, the only way the combination could be true is if I could answer "yes" (true) to both of the questions "Do you want french fries?" and "Do you want a baked potato?" The resulting combinations of possibilities are collectively known as a *truth table*; the truth table for **&&** appears in Listing 2.8.

Listing 2.8: The truth table for && ("and").

```
> true && true
true
> false && true
false
> true && false
false
> false && false
false
```

We can apply this to a conditional as shown in Listing 2.9.

Listing 2.9: Using the && operator in a conditional.

```
> let x = "foo";
> let y = "";
> if (x.length === 0 && y.length === 0) {
    "Both strings are empty!";
  } else {
    "At least one of the strings is nonempty.";
  }
'At least one of the strings is nonempty.'
```

In Listing 2.9, **y.length** is in fact **0**, but **x.length** isn't, so the combination is **false** (in agreement with Listing 2.8), and JavaScript evaluates the **else** branch.

In contrast to **&&**, **||** lets us take action if *either* comparison (or both) is true (Listing 2.10).

Listing 2.10: The truth table for **||** ("or").

```
> true || true
true
> true || false
true
> false || true
true
> false || false
false
```

We can use **||** in a conditional as shown in Listing 2.11.

Listing 2.11: Using the **||** operator in a conditional.

```
> if (x.length === 0 || y.length === 0) {
    "At least one of the strings is empty!";
  } else {
    "Neither of the strings is empty.";
  }
'At least one of the strings is empty!'
```

Note from Listing 2.10 that **||** isn't *exclusive*, meaning that the result is true even when *both* statements are true. This stands in contrast to colloquial usage, where a

Figure 2.8: Turns out I only wanted fries.

statement like "I want fries or a baked potato" implies that you want either fries *or* a baked potato, but you don't want both (Figure 2.8).[8]

In addition to **&&** and **||**, JavaScript supports *negation* via the "not" operator **!** (often pronounced "bang"), which just converts **true** to **false** and **false** to **true** (Listing 2.12).

Listing 2.12: The truth table for !.

```
> !true
false
> !false
true
```

We can use **!** in a conditional as shown in Listing 2.13.

8. Image courtesy of Rikaphoto/Shutterstock.

Listing 2.13: Using the ! operator in a conditional.

```
> if (!(x.length === 0)) {
  "x is not empty.";
} else {
  "x is empty.";
}
'x is not empty.'
```

The code in Listing 2.13 is valid JavaScript, as it simply negates the test **x.length === 0**, yielding **true**:

```
> (!(x.length === 0))
true
```

In this case, though, it's more common to use **!==** ("not equals"):

```
> if (x.length !== 0) {
    "x is not empty.";
  } else {
  "x is empty.";
  }
'x is not empty'
```

2.4.2 Bang Bang

Not all booleans are the result of comparisons, and in fact every JavaScript object has a value of either **true** or **false** in a boolean context. We can force JavaScript to use such a boolean context with **!!** (pronounced "bang bang"); because **!** converts between **true** and **false**, using *two* exclamation points returns us back to the original boolean:

```
> !!true
true
> !!false
false
```

Using this trick allows us to see that a string like **"foo"** is **true** in a boolean context:

```
> !!"foo"
true
```

As it happens, the empty string is *false* in a boolean context:[9]

```
> !!""
false
```

As a result, we can rewrite code like Listing 2.9 more compactly by omitting the length comparison (while negating **x** and **y**), as shown in Listing 2.14.

Listing 2.14: Using a conditional to force a boolean context.

```
> if (!x && !y) {
    "Both strings are empty!";
  } else {
    "At least one of the strings is nonempty.";
  }
'At least one of the strings is nonempty.'
```

2.4.3 Exercises

1. If **x** is **"foo"** and **y** is **""** (the empty string), what is the value of **x && y**? Verify using the "bang bang" notation that **x && y** is false in a boolean context. *Hint*: When applying **!!** to a compound expression, wrap the whole thing in parentheses.

2. What is **x || y**? What is it in a boolean context? Rewrite Listing 2.14 to use **x || y**, ensuring that the result is the same. (*Hint*: Switch the order of the strings.)

2.5 Methods

As noted in Section 2.4, JavaScript string objects have only one property (**length**), but they support a wide variety of methods.[10] In the language of object-oriented programming, a particular string, or *string instance*, is said to "respond to" a particular method, indicated using the dot notation first seen in Section 1.3.1.

---

9. This is the sort of detail that varies from language to language. In Ruby, for example, even the empty string is **true** in a boolean context.

10. Recall from Section 1.3.1 that a method is a particular kind of function, one attached to an object and invoked using the dot notation.

Figure 2.9: This honey badger used to be a HONEY BADGER, but he don't care.

For example, strings respond to the instance method **toLowerCase()**, which (surprise!) converts the string to all lowercase letters (Figure 2.9):[11]

```
$ node
> "HONEY BADGER".toLowerCase();
'honey badger'
```

This is the sort of method that could be useful, for example, when standardizing on lowercase letters in an email address:[12]

```
> let username = firstName.toLowerCase();
> `${username}@example.com`;    // Sample email address
'michael@example.com'
```

Note that, in contrast to the **length** property, a method has to be called with arguments, even if there aren't any. That's why

---

11. Image courtesy of Pavel Kovaricek/Shutterstock.

12. If you've exited and re-entered your Node console, **firstName** might no longer be defined, as such definitions don't persist from session to session. If this is the case, apply your technical sophistication (Box 1.1) to figure out what to do.

Figure 2.10: Early typesetters kept large letters in the "upper case" and small letters in the "lower case".

```
toLowerCase()
```

ends with opening and closing parentheses: **toLowerCase** is a function that takes zero arguments. Also note that official JavaScript string methods follow the same capitalization convention (CamelCase with a lowercase letter to start) that we introduced ourselves in Section 2.2.

As you might be able to guess, JavaScript supports the opposite operation as well; before looking at the example below, see if you can guess the method for converting a string to uppercase (Figure 2.10).[13]

I'm betting you got the right answer:

```
> lastName.toUpperCase();
'HARTL'
```

---

13. Image courtesy of arco1/123RF.

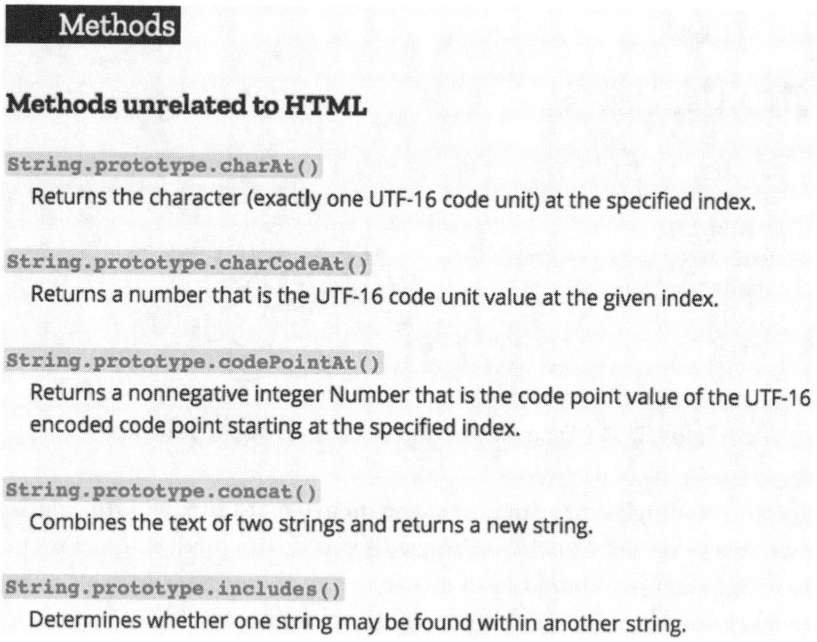

Methods

Methods unrelated to HTML

`String.prototype.charAt()`
  Returns the character (exactly one UTF-16 code unit) at the specified index.

`String.prototype.charCodeAt()`
  Returns a number that is the UTF-16 code unit value at the given index.

`String.prototype.codePointAt()`
  Returns a nonnegative integer Number that is the code point value of the UTF-16 encoded code point starting at the specified index.

`String.prototype.concat()`
  Combines the text of two strings and returns a new string.

`String.prototype.includes()`
  Determines whether one string may be found within another string.

Figure 2.11: Some JavaScript string methods.

Being able to guess answers like this is a hallmark of technical sophistication, but as noted in Box 1.1 another key skill is being able to use the documentation. In particular, the Mozilla Developer Network page on **String** objects has a long list of useful string instance methods.[14] Let's take a look at some of them (Figure 2.11).

Inspecting the methods in Figure 2.11, we see on the bottom some code that looks like this:

```
String.prototype.includes()
```

followed by a brief description. What does **String.prototype** mean here? We'll find out in Chapter 7, but the real answer is *we don't have to know exactly what it means to use the documentation.* Selective ignorance is classic technical sophistication.

---

14. You can find such pages by going directly to the MDN website (https://developer.mozilla.org/en-US/docs/Web/JavaScript), but the truth is that I nearly always find such pages by Googling things like "javascript string".

Examples

Using `includes()`

```
1   var str = 'To be, or not to be, that is the question.';
2
3   console.log(str.includes('To be'));        // true
4   console.log(str.includes('question'));     // true
5   console.log(str.includes('nonexistent'));  // false
6   console.log(str.includes('To be', 1));     // false
7   console.log(str.includes('TO BE'));        // false
```

Figure 2.12: Examples for the string `includes()` method.

Clicking through on the `String.prototype.includes()` link and scrolling down shows us a bunch of examples (Figure 2.12). Notice that, as prophesied in Section 2.2, the use of **var** instead of **let** is very common; being able to tolerate these slight mismatches is yet another application of technical sophistication.

Let's try out the examples shown in Figure 2.12, with the following modifications:

1. Use **let** instead of **var**.
2. Use **soliloquy** instead of **str**.
3. Use double-quoted strings instead of single-quoted strings.
4. Change the quote to use a colon as in the original (Figure 2.13).[15]
5. Omit the use of **console.log**.
6. Omit the current comments, while adding some of our own.

The result in a Node REPL looks something like Listing 2.15.

Listing 2.15: Includes or does not include? That is the question.

```
> let soliloquy = "To be, or not to be, that is the question:";
> soliloquy.includes("To be");      // Does it include the substring "To be"?
true
> soliloquy.includes("question");   // What about "question"?
```

15. Image courtesy of Everett Collection/Shutterstock.

Figure 2.13: Hamlet, Prince of Denmark, asks: "To be, or not to be, that is the question."

```
true
> soliloquy.includes("nonexistent");   // This string doesn't appear.
false
> soliloquy.includes("TO BE");         // String inclusion is case-sensitive.
false
> soliloquy.includes("To be", 1);      // Can you guess what this one means?
false
> soliloquy.includes("o be,", 1);      // A hint for the previous one
true
```

Of the lines in Listing 2.15, the only two that you might not be able to figure out right away are the last two. You'll find the solution to this mystery, as well as pointers to some other common string methods, in the section exercises.

2.5.1 Exercises

1. Write the JavaScript code to test whether the string "hoNeY BaDGer" includes the string "badger" without regard to case.

2. What does **includes(string, i)** do for any integer **i**? *Hint*: Counting in JavaScript starts at **0** rather than **1**.

2.6 String Iteration

Our final topic on strings is *iteration*, which is the practice of repeatedly stepping through an object one element at a time. Iteration is a common theme in computer programming, and we'll see some other examples later in this tutorial (Section 3.5 and Section 5.4). We'll also see how one sign of your growing power as a developer is learning how to *avoid* iteration entirely (as discussed in Chapter 6 and Section 8.5).

In the case of strings, we'll be learning how to iterate one *character* at a time. There are two main prerequisites to this: First, we need to learn how to access a particular character in a string, and second, we need to learn how to make a *loop*.

We can figure out how to access a particular string character by consulting the list of **String** methods (https://developer.mozilla.org/en-US/docs/Web/JavaScript /Reference/Global_Objects/String), which includes the following entry:

String.prototype.charAt()
Returns the character (exactly one UTF-16 code unit) at the specified index.

Drilling down into the documentation (https://developer.mozilla.org/en-US/docs /Web/JavaScript/Reference/Global_Objects/String/charAt) for the method itself, we see from the examples what **charAt** and "index" mean in this context. Using the **soliloquy** string from Section 2.5, we can illustrate this as shown in Listing 2.16.

Listing 2.16: Investigating the behavior of **charAt**.

```
> console.log(soliloquy);    // Just a reminder of what the string is
To be, or not to be, that is the question:
> soliloquy.charAt(0);
'T'
> soliloquy.charAt(1);
'o'
> soliloquy.charAt(2);
' '
```

We see in Listing 2.16 that **charAt(0)** returns the first character, **charAt(1)** returns the second, and so on. (We'll discuss this possibly counter-intuitive numbering convention, called "zero-offset", further in Section 3.1.) Each number **0**, **1**, **2**, etc., is called an *index* (plural *indexes* or *indices*).

Now let's look at our first example of a loop. In particular, we'll use a **for** loop that defines an index value **i** and increments its value until it reaches some maximum (Listing 2.17).

Listing 2.17: A simple **for** loop.

```
> for (let i = 0; i < 5; i++) {
    console.log(i);
}
0
1
2
3
4
```

This sort of loop (with only minor variations in syntax) is common across an astonishing variety of programming languages, from C and C++ to Java, Perl, PHP, and (as we've just seen) JavaScript. Listing 2.17 shows how, after using **let** to create **i** and set it to **0**, the index variable gets incremented by **1** until it reaches **5**, at which point **i < 5** is **false** and the loop stops. The notation **i++**, meanwhile, is an *increment* statement that bumps up the value of **i** by one at a time.

If you find the code in Listing 2.17 confusing or ugly, you're in good company. I consider it a hallmark of good programming to *avoid* using **for** loops as much as possible, preferring instead **forEach** loops (Section 5.4) or avoiding loops entirely using functional programming (Chapter 6 and Section 8.5). As computer scientist (and personal friend) Mike Vanier (Figure 2.14) once put it in an email to Paul Graham:

> This [tedious repetition] grinds you down after a while; if I had a nickel for every time I've written "for (i = 0; i < N; i++)" in C I'd be a millionaire.

Note how the **for** loop syntax in Mike's email is almost identical to that in Listing 2.17; the only differences are the absence of **let** and the use of **N**, which we can infer from context represents some upper bound on the loop's index.

Figure 2.14: Just a few more **for** loops and Mike Vanier will be a millionaire.

We'll see how to avoid getting ground down starting in Chapter 6, but for now Listing 2.17 is the best we can do.

Let's combine Listing 2.16 and Listing 2.17 to iterate through all the characters in the first line of Hamlet's famous soliloquy. The only new thing we need is the index for when the loop should stop. In Listing 2.17, we hard-coded the upper limit (**i <
5**), and we could do the same here if we wanted. The **soliloquy** variable is a bit long to count the characters by hand, though, so let's ask JavaScript to tell us using the **length** property (Section 2.4):

```
> soliloquy.length
42
```

This exceptionally auspicious result suggests writing code like this:

```
for (let i = 0; i < 42; i++) {
  console.log(soliloquy.charAt(i));
}
```

This code will work, and it is in perfect analogy with Listing 2.17, but it also raises a question: Why hard-code the length when we can just use the **length** property in the loop itself?

The answer is that we shouldn't, and when looping it's common practice to use the **length** property whenever possible. The resulting improved **for** loop (with result) appears in Listing 2.18.

Listing 2.18: Combining **charAt** and a **for** loop.

```
> for (let i = 0; i < soliloquy.length; i++) {
  console.log(soliloquy.charAt(i));
}
T
o

b
e
.
.
.
t
i
o
n
:
```

As noted above, **for** loops are best avoided if at all possible, but this less elegant style of looping is still an excellent place to start. As we'll see in Chapter 8, one powerful technique is to write a *test* for the functionality we want, then get it passing any way we can, and then *refactor* the code to use a more elegant method. The second step in this process (called *test-driven development*, or TDD) often involves writing inelegant but easy-to-understand code—a task at which the humble **for** loop excels.

2.6.1 Exercises

1. Use **let** to define a variable **N** that's equal to the length of **soliloquy**, and show that the code in Mike Vanier's **for** loop actually works in JavaScript exactly as written. (In particular, you can sometimes get away with omitting **let**, though this isn't a good practice.)

2. Show that you can replace the **charAt** method in Listing 2.18 with a literal bracket notation, like this: **soliloquy[i]**.

CHAPTER 3

Arrays

In Chapter 2, we saw that strings can be thought of as sequences of characters in a particular order. In this chapter, we'll learn about the *array* data type, which is the general JavaScript container for arbitrary elements in a particular order. We'll start by explicitly connecting strings and arrays via the String **split** method (Section 3.1), and then learn about various array methods throughout the rest of the chapter.

3.1 Splitting

So far we've spent a lot of time understanding strings, and there's a natural way to get from strings to arrays via the **split** method:

```
> "ant bat cat".split(" ");      // Split a string into a three-element array.
[ 'ant', 'bat', 'cat' ]
```

We see from this result that **split** returns a list of the strings that are separated from each other by a space in the original string.

Splitting on space is one of the most common operations, but we can split on nearly anything else as well:

```
> "ant,bat,cat".split(",");
[ 'ant', 'bat', 'cat' ]
> "ant, bat, cat".split(", ");
[ 'ant', 'bat', 'cat' ]
> "antheybatheycat".split("hey");
[ 'ant', 'bat', 'cat' ]
```

We can even split a string into its component characters by splitting on the empty string:

```
> "badger".split("")
[ 'b', 'a', 'd', 'g', 'e', 'r' ]
```

We'll put this basic technique to good use in Section 5.3 (and we'll also discover it has an important limitation).

Finally, it's worth noting that splitting supports *regular expressions*, which are covered in Section 4.3.

3.1.1 Exercises

1. Assign **a** to the result of splitting the string "A man, a plan, a canal, Panama" on comma-space. How many elements does the resulting array have?

2. Can you guess the method to reverse **a** in place? (Google around if necessary.)

3.2 Array Access

Having connected strings with arrays via the **split** method, we'll now discover a second close connection as well. Let's start by assigning a variable to an array of characters created using **split**:

```
> let a = "badger".split("");
```

We can access particular elements of **a** using a bracket notation that's common to a huge number of different languages, as seen in Listing 3.1.

Listing 3.1: Array access with the bracket notation.

```
> a[0];
'b'
> a[1];
'a'
> a[2];
'd'
```

Does Listing 3.1 look a little familiar? It's the same basic relationship between characters and numerical index that we saw with the **String#charAt** method in Listing 2.16. (The notation in the previous sentence indicates that **charAt** is an *instance method*, i.e., a method on string instances.) In fact, the bracket notation actually works directly on strings:

```
> "badger"[0];
'b'
> "badger"[1];
'a'
```

We see from Listing 3.1 that, as with strings, arrays are *zero-offset*, meaning that the "first" element has index **0**, the second has index **1**, and so on. This convention can be confusing, and in fact it's common to refer to the initial element for zero-offset arrays as the "zeroth" element as a reminder that the indexing starts at **0**. This convention can also be confusing when using multiple languages (some of which start array indexing at **1**), as illustrated in the xkcd comic strip "Donald Knuth" (https://m.xkcd.com/163/).[1]

So far we've dealt exclusively with arrays of characters, but JavaScript arrays can contain all kinds of elements:

```
> a = ["badger", 42, soliloquy.includes("To be")];
[ 'badger', 42, true ]
> a[2];
true
> a[3];
undefined
```

We see here that the square bracket access notation works as usual for an array of mixed types, which shouldn't come as a surprise. We also see that trying to access an array index outside of the defined range returns **undefined** (a value which we saw before in the context of **console.log** (Figure 2.4)). This might be a surprise if you have previous programming experience, since many languages raise an error if you try to access an element that's out of range, but JavaScript is more tolerant in this regard.

---

1. This particular xkcd strip takes its name from renowned computer scientist Donald Knuth (pronounced "kuh-NOOTH"), author of *The Art of Computer Programming* and creator of the TEX typesetting system used to prepare many technical documents, including this one.

3.2.1 Exercises

1. Write a **for** loop to print out the characters obtained from splitting "honey badger" on the empty string.

2. See if you can guess the value of **undefined** in a boolean context. Use **!!** to confirm.

3.3 Array Slicing

In addition to supporting the bracket notation described in Section 3.2, JavaScript supports a technique known as *array slicing* for accessing multiple elements at a time. In anticipation of learning to *sort* in Section 3.4, let's redefine our array **a** to have purely numerical elements:

```
> a = [42, 8, 17, 99];
[ 42, 8, 17, 99 ]
```

The simplest way to slice an array is to provide only one argument, which returns all the elements in the array from that index on. For example, for an array with four elements, **slice(1)** returns the second, third, and fourth ones (recall that the "first" or zeroth element has index **0**):

```
> a.slice(1);
[ 8, 17, 99 ]
```

We can also slice from one index to another:

```
> a.slice(1, 3);
[ 8, 17 ]
```

Slicing gives us an easy way to perform a common task, which is to access the last element in an array. Arrays, like strings, have a **length** property, so we could find the last element like this:

```
> a.length;
4
> a[a.length-1];
99
```

This can get a little messy if the variable name is long, though, which often happens
in bigger projects that have lots of variables:

```
> let aMuchLongerArrayName = a;
> aMuchLongerArrayName[aMuchLongerArrayName.length - 1];
99
```

This leads us to a second method for picking off the last element, which is to use
slice with a *negative* number, which counts from the end:

```
> aMuchLongerArrayName.slice(-1);
[ 99 ]
```

This is an array with one element, so we can select the element itself using the bracket
notation:

```
> aMuchLongerArrayName.slice(-1)[0];
99
```

A final common case is where we want to access the final element and remove it
at the same time. We'll cover the method for doing this in Section 3.4.2.

3.3.1 Exercises

1. Define an array with the numbers 1 through 10. Use slicing and **length** to select
   the third element through the third-to-last. Accomplish the same task using a
   negative index.
2. Show that strings also support the **slice** method by selecting just **bat** from the
   string **"ant bat cat"**. (You might have to experiment a little to get the indices
   just right.)

3.4 More Array Methods

In addition to the **slice** method seen in Section 3.3, arrays respond to a wealth
of other methods. As usual, the documentation (https://developer.mozilla.org/en-
US/docs/Web/JavaScript/Reference/Global_Objects/Array) is a good place to go
for details.

As with strings, arrays respond to an **includes** method to test for element inclusion:

```
> a;
[ 42, 8, 17, 99 ]
> a.includes(42);          // Test for element inclusion.
true
> a.includes("foo");
false
```

3.4.1 Sorting and Reversing

You can also sort an array in place—an excellent trick that in ye olden days of C often required a custom implementation. In JavaScript, we just call **sort()**:

```
> a.sort();
[ 17, 42, 8, 99 ]
> a;                       // `a` has changed as the result of `sort()`.
[ 17, 42, 8, 99 ]
```

You might notice something strange here, which is that JavaScript has sorted the elements of the array not according to their numerical values, but rather "alphabetically", so that **17** comes before **8** because **1** comes before **8** in the ordering scheme (ASCII) used by computers. (We'll learn how to sort arrays numerically in Chapter 5.)

Another useful method—one we'll put to good use in developing our palindrome theme starting in Section 5.3—is the **reverse** method:

```
> a.reverse();
[ 99, 8, 42, 17 ]
> a;                       // Like `sort()`, `reverse()` mutates the array.
[ 99, 8, 42, 17 ]
```

As noted in the comment, methods like **a.sort()** and **a.reverse()** *mutate* the array, meaning they modify it as a side effect of performing their respective actions. This is the sort of behavior that varies from one programming language to the next, so be careful when using similar methods in other languages.

3.4.2 Pushing and Popping

One useful pair of array methods is **push** and **pop**; **push** lets us append an element to the end of an array, while **pop** removes it:

```
> a.push(6);                    // Pushing onto an array (returns new length)
5
> a;
[ 99, 8, 42, 17, 6 ]
> a.push("foo");
6
> a;
[ 99, 8, 42, 17, 6, 'foo' ]
> a.pop();                      // `pop` returns the value itself
'foo'
> a.pop();
6
> a;
[ 99, 8, 42, 17 ]
```

As noted in the comments, **pop** returns the value of the final element (while removing it as a side effect), but **push** (somewhat counter-intuitively) returns the *length* of the new array. As of this writing, I don't know why (and neither does Stack Overflow).

We are now in a position to appreciate the comment made in Section 3.3 about obtaining the last element of the array, as long as we don't mind mutating it:

```
> let lastElement = a.pop();
> lastElement;
17
> a;
[ 99, 8, 42 ]
> let theAnswerToLifeTheUniverseAndEverything = a.pop();
```

3.4.3 Undoing a Split

A final example of an array method, one that brings us full circle from Section 3.1, is **join**. Just as **split** splits a string into array elements, **join** joins array elements into a string (Listing 3.2).

Listing 3.2: Different ways to join.

```
> a = ["ant", "bat", "cat", 42];
[ 'ant', 'bat', 'cat', 42 ]
> a.join();                      // Join on default (comma).
'ant,bat,cat,42'
> a.join(", ");                  // Join on comma-space.
'ant, bat, cat, 42'
> a.join(" -- ");                // Join on double dashes.
'ant -- bat -- cat -- 42'
> a.join("");                    // Join on empty space.
'antbatcat42'
```

Note that **42**, which is an integer, is automatically converted to a string in the join.

3.4.4 Exercises

1. The **split** and **join** methods are almost inverse operations, but not quite. In particular, confirm using == (*not* ===) that **a.join(" ").split(" ")** in Listing 3.2 is *not* the same as **a**. Why not?

2. Using the array documentation, figure out how to push onto or pop off the *front* of an array. *Hint*: The names aren't intuitive at all, so you might have to work a bit.

3.5 Array Iteration

One of the most common tasks with arrays is iterating through their elements and performing an operation with each one. This might sound familiar, since we solved the exact same problem with strings in Section 2.6, and indeed the solution is virtually the same. All we need to do is adapt the **for** loop from Listing 2.18 to arrays.

We could get there in one step fairly easily, but the connection is even clearer if we first rewrite the string **for** loop using the bracket access notation, which (as we saw in Section 3.2) works on strings as well. The result for the **soliloquy** string defined in Listing 2.15 is shown in Listing 3.3.

Listing 3.3: Combining string access and a **for** loop.

```
> for (let i = 0; i < soliloquy.length; i++) {
   console.log(soliloquy[i]);
}
T
o

b
e
.
.
.
t
i
o
n
:
```

The result in Listing 3.3 is exactly the same as that shown in Listing 2.18.

The application of this pattern to arrays should now be clear. All we need to do is replace **soliloquy** with **a**, as shown in Listing 3.4; the rest of the code is identical.

Listing 3.4: Combining array access and a **for** loop.

```
> for (let i = 0; i < a.length; i++) {
     console.log(a[i]);
   }
ant
bat
cat
42
```

One thing worth noting here is that the iteration index variable **i** appears in both **for** loops. As you may recall if you completed the exercises in Section 2.2.2, redefining a variable that's already been declared with **let** generally results in an error. Why were we able to reuse **i** in this context?

The answer is that in the context of a **for** loop the *scope* of the variable is restricted to the loop, and disappears when the loop is finished.

Figure 3.1: Mike Vanier is still annoyed by typing out **for** loops.

That's convenient, but it's not the best way to iterate through arrays, and Mike Vanier still wouldn't be happy (Figure 3.1). We'll see a cleaner method for iterating through arrays in Section 5.4, and a way of avoiding iteration entirely in Chapter 6.

3.5.1 Exercises

1. Show that the identifier **i** is undefined both before and after a **for** loop executes. (You might have to exit and re-enter the Node console.)

2. Define an accumulator variable **total** and combine it with a loop to add all the elements of Listing 3.4. You can use the code in Listing 3.5 to get started (just replace the comment with the proper code). How does the value of **total** compare to **a.join("")**?

Listing 3.5: Skeleton for calculating a total.

```
> let total = "";
> for (let i = 0; i < a.length; i++) {
    // set total equal to the running total plus the current element
  }
```

CHAPTER 4

Other Native Objects

Now that we've taken a look at strings and arrays, we'll continue with a tour of some other important JavaScript objects: math, dates, regular expressions, and generic objects.

4.1 Math and Number

Like most programming languages, JavaScript supports a large number of mathematical operations:

```
> 1 + 1;
2
> 2 - 3;
-1
> 2 * 3;
6
> 10/5;
2
> 2/3;
0.6666666666666666
```

Note that the final example here isn't exact; it's a *floating-point* number (also called a *float*), which can't be represented exactly by the computer. But in fact JavaScript has only one numerical type, and even something like **1** or **2** is treated as floating point under the hood. This is convenient for us as programmers, since it means we never have to make distinctions between different kinds of numbers.[1]

Many programmers, including me, find it convenient to fire up a REPL and use it as a simple calculator when the need arises. It's not fancy, but it's quick and relatively powerful, and the ability to define variables often comes in handy as well.

4.1.1   More Advanced Operations

JavaScript supports more advanced mathematical operations via a *global object* called **Math**, which has properties and methods for things like mathematical constants, exponentiation (powers),[2] roots, and trigonometric functions:

```
> Math.PI
3.141592653589793
> Math.pow(2, 3);
8
> Math.sqrt(3)
1.7320508075688772
> Math.cos(2*Math.PI)
1
```

There is one gotcha for those coming from high-school (and even college) text-books that use ln for the natural logarithm. Like mathematicians and most other programming languages, JavaScript uses log instead:

```
> Math.E;
2.718281828459045
> Math.log(Math.E);
1
> Math.log(10);
2.302585092994046
```

Mathematicians typically indicate base-ten logarithms using $\log_{10}$, and JavaScript follows suit with **log10**:

---

1. In contrast to JavaScript, many languages distinguish between integers and floats, which leads to pitfalls like **1.0/2.0** being the expected **0.5**, but **1/2** being **0**.

2. Adding support for exponentiation with two asterisks ****** is in the works but isn't universally implemented as of this writing.

```
> Math.log10(10);
1
> Math.log10(1000000);
6
> Math.log10(Math.E);
0.4342944819032518
```

The Math documentation (https://developer.mozilla.org/en–US/docs/Web/JavaScript/Reference/Global_Objects/Math) includes a more comprehensive list of further operations.

4.1.2 Math to String

We discussed in Chapter 3 how to get from strings to arrays (and vice versa) using **split** and **join**. Similarly, JavaScript allows us to convert between numbers and strings.

Probably the most common way to convert from a number to a string is using the **toString()** method, as we can see with this useful definition (https://tauday.com/tau–manifesto) (Figure 4.1):[3]

```
> let tau = 2 * Math.PI;
> tau.toString();
'6.283185307179586'
```

The **toString()** method won't work on a bare integer:

```
> 100.toString();
100.toString();
^^^^

SyntaxError: Invalid or unexpected token
```

But it will work if you use an extra dot, so that JavaScript treats the number as a float:

```
> 100.0.toString()
'100'
```

---

3. The use of τ to represent the circle constant $6.283185\ldots$ was proposed in a math essay I published in 2010 called *The Tau Manifesto*, which also established a math holiday called Tau Day (https://tauday.com/), celebrated annually on June 28.

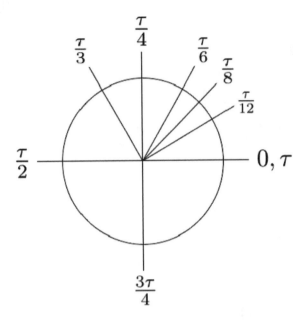

Figure 4.1: Some special angles in terms of $\tau = 2\pi$.

This is unfortunate behavior, since the string corresponding to **100.0** should more properly be **"100.0"**, but this is a price we pay for JavaScript's lack of a proper integer data type.

Another way to convert raw numbers to strings is to use the **String** object directly:

```
> String(100.0);
'100.0'
> String(tau);
'6.283185307179586'
```

We see from the second example that **String** also works on variables.

This method of converting to strings dovetails nicely with going the opposite direction, which uses the **Number** object directly:

```
> Number("6.283185307179586");
6.283185307179586
> String(Number("6.283185307179586"));
```

```
'6.283185307179586'
> Number('1.24e6')
1240000
```

We see in the final line that JavaScript supports scientific notation:

```
> 1.24e6
1240000
```

4.1.3 Exercises

1. See if you can guess the return value of **String(Number('1.24e6'))**. Confirm using the Node REPL.

2. Like most programming languages, JavaScript lacks support for imaginary numbers, i.e., numbers that are a real multiple of the *imaginary unit i* (satisfying the equation $i^2 = -1$, sometimes written as $i = \sqrt{-1}$). What is the JavaScript value of the square root of -1? By guessing or Googling, figure out what this value stands for. What is its boolean value?

4.2 Dates

Another frequently used built-in object is **Date**, which represents a single moment in time.

The **Date** object gives us our first chance to use the **new** function, a so-called *constructor function* that is the standard JavaScript way to create a new object. So far, we've been able to rely on "literal constructors" like quotes and square brackets, but we can also define things like strings and arrays using **new**:

```
> let s = new String("A man, a plan, a canal—Panama!");
> s;
[String: 'A man, a plan, a canal—Panama!']
> s.split(", ");
[ 'A man', 'a plan', 'a canal—Panama!' ]
```

and

```
> let a = new Array();
> a.push(3);
```

```
1
> a.push(4);
2
> a.push("hello, world!");
3
> a;
[ 3, 4, 'hello, world!' ]
> a.pop();
'hello, world!'
```

Unlike strings and arrays, dates have no literal constructor, so we *have* to use **new** in this case:

```
> let now = new Date();
> now;
2022-03-16T 19:22:13.673Z
> let moonLanding = new Date("July 20, 1969 20:18");
> now - moonLanding;
1661616253673
```

The result here is the number of milliseconds since the day and time of the first Moon landing (Figure 4.2).[4] (Your results, of course, will vary, because time marches on, and your value for **new Date()** will differ.)

As with other JavaScript objects, **Date** objects respond to a variety of methods:

```
> now.getYear();        // Gives a weird answer
122
> now.getFullYear();    // This is what we want instead.
2022
> now.getMonth();
2
> now.getDay();
3
```

The first line here shows that sometimes the results of JavaScript methods are confusing, so it's important to be wary and double-check the values by hand from time to time.

Things like the month and day are returned as indices, and like everything in JavaScript they are zero-offset. For example, month **0** is January, month **1** is February, month **2** is March, etc.

---

4. Image courtesy of Castleski/Shutterstock.

Figure 4.2: Buzz Aldrin and Neil Armstrong somehow got to the Moon (and back!) without JavaScript.

Even though the official international standard is that Monday is the first day, JavaScript follows the American convention of using Sunday instead. We can get the name of the day by making an array of strings for the days of the week, and then using **getDay()** as an index in the array with the square bracket notation (Section 3.1):

```
> let daysOfTheWeek = ["Sunday", "Monday", "Tuesday", "Wednesday",
                       "Thursday", "Friday", "Saturday"];
> daysOfTheWeek[now.getDay()];
'Wednesday'
```

Your results will vary, of course, unless you happen to be reading this on a Wednesday.

As a final exercise, let's update our web page with an alert including the day of the week. The code appears in Listing 4.1, with the result as shown in Figure 4.3.

Listing 4.1: Adding a greeting customized to the day of the week.

index.html

```
<!DOCTYPE html>
<html>
  <head>
    <title>Learn Enough JavaScript</title>
    <meta charset="utf-8">
    <script>
      const daysOfTheWeek = ["Sunday", "Monday", "Tuesday", "Wednesday",
                             "Thursday", "Friday", "Saturday"];
      let now = new Date();
      let dayName = daysOfTheWeek[now.getDay()];
      alert(`Hello, world! Happy ${dayName}.`);
    </script>
  </head>
  <body>

  </body>
</html>
```

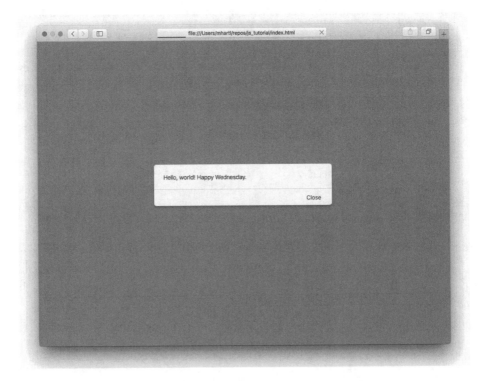

Figure 4.3: A greeting customized just for today.

Note that Listing 4.1 uses **const** instead of **let** when defining **daysOfTheWeek**:

```
const daysOfTheWeek = ["Sunday", "Monday", "Tuesday", "Wednesday",
                       "Thursday", "Friday", "Saturday"];
```

Here **const**, which (as you can probably guess) is short for "constant", gives us a way to indicate that the value of the variable won't change.[5] Some people even go so far as to use **const** in preference to **let** whenever possible. My preference is to use **let** as a default, and to use **const** as a signal that it's especially important for the value not to change.

4.2.1   Exercises

1. Create a new **Date** object by passing it a string for your birthday (including year). JavaScript supports a number of different formats, so it will probably work with whichever date format you prefer. Pretty cool, no?

2. How many seconds after the Moon landing were you born? (Or maybe you were even born *before* the Moon landing—in which case, lucky you! I hope you got to watch it on TV.)

4.3   Regular Expressions

JavaScript has full support for *regular expressions*, often called *regexes* or *regexps* for short, which are a powerful mini-language for matching patterns in text. A full mastery of regular expressions is beyond the scope of this book (and perhaps beyond the scope of human ability), but the good news is that there are many resources available for learning about them incrementally. (Some such resources are mentioned in "Grepping" (https://www.learnenough.com/command-line-tutorial/inspecting_files) in *Learn Enough Command Line to Be Dangerous* (https://www.learnenough.com/command-line) and "Global find and replace" (https://www.learnenough.com/text-editor-tutorial/advanced_text_editing#sec-global_find_and_replace) in *Learn Enough Text Editor to Be Dangerous* (https://www.learnenough.com/text-editor).) The most

---

5. Technically, **const** creates an *immutable binding*—i.e., the name can't change, but the value can. Mutating the contents of a variable created using **const** is a bad practice, though, and should be avoided to prevent confusion.

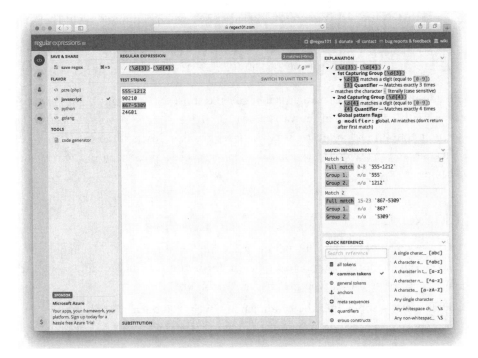

Figure 4.4: An online regex builder.

important thing to know about is the general idea of regular expressions; you can fill in the details as you go along.

Regexes are notoriously terse and error-prone; as programmer Jamie Zawinski famously said:

> Some people, when confronted with a problem, think "I know, I'll use regular expressions." Now they have two problems.

Luckily, this situation is greatly ameliorated by web applications like regex101 (https://regex101.com/), which let us build up regexes interactively (Figure 4.4). Moreover, such resources typically include a quick reference to assist us in finding the code for matching particular patterns (Figure 4.5).

If you look carefully at Figure 4.4, you might be able to see the checkmark in the menu on the left indicating that "javascript" has been selected for the regex input format. This arranges to use the exact regular expression conventions we need

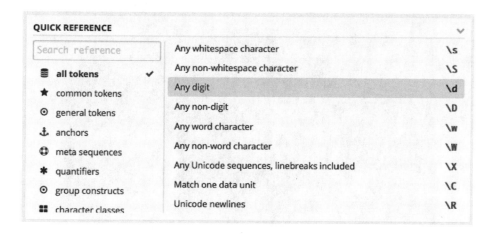

Figure 4.5: A close-up of the regex reference.

in this tutorial. In practice, languages differ little in their implementation of regular expressions, but it's wise to use the correct language-specific settings, and always to double-check when moving a regex to a different language.

Let's take a look at some simple regex matches in JavaScript. Our examples will draw on both the regex methods and string methods specialized for regexes. (The latter are often more convenient in practice.)

4.3.1 Regex Methods

A basic regex consists of a sequence of characters that matches a particular pattern. We can create a new regex using the **new** function (Section 4.2) on the **RegExp** object. For example, here's a regex that matches standard American ZIP codes (Figure 4.6),[6] consisting of five digits in a row:

```
> let zipCode = new RegExp("\\d{5}");
```

Here **\d** represents any digit (0–9), and the first backslash is needed to *escape* the second backslash to get a literal backslash in the string. (We'll see how to avoid

---

6. Image courtesy of 4kclips/123RF.

Figure 4.6: 90210 is one of the most expensive ZIP codes in America.

this inconvenient requirement using a literal regex constructor in Section 4.3.2.) Meanwhile, **{5}** says to match exactly five digits in a row.

If you use regular expressions a lot, eventually you'll memorize many of these rules, but you can always look them up in a quick reference (Figure 4.5).

Now let's see how to tell if a string matches a regex. Regular expressions come with an **exec** method that "executes" the regex on a string:

```
> let result = zipCode.exec("Beverly Hills 90210");
> result;
[ '90210', index: 14, input: 'Beverly Hills 90210' ]
```

The result here includes the matching string, the index number where the match starts, and the original input.

I don't like the format of the result above, mainly because the output is a weird and confusing pseudo-array that seemingly has three elements but in fact has length **1**:

```
> result.length
1
```

4.3.2 String Methods

A more convenient way to make regex matches is to use string methods. There's also a literal regex constructor syntax that's more convenient for most purposes.

As we learned in Section 4.2, some JavaScript objects need to be created using **new**, while others have optional literal constructors, such as quotes for making strings and square brackets for making arrays. Regexes support just such a literal constructor syntax, namely, patterns inside forward slashes:

```
> zipCode = /\d{5}/;
/\d{5}/
```

Note that, unlike in the case of the named **RegExp** constructor in Section 4.3.1, when using the literal constructor we don't have to escape the **\d** with an extra backslash.

Now let's build up a longer string with multiple ZIP codes (Figure 4.7):[7]

```
> let s = "Beverly Hills 90210 was a '90s TV show set in Los Angeles.";
> s += " 91125 is another ZIP code in the Los Angeles area."
'Beverly Hills 90210 was a \'90s TV show set in Los Angeles. 91125 is another
 ZIP code in the Los Angeles area.'
```

You should be able to use your technical sophistication (Box 1.1) to infer what the **+=** operator does here if you haven't seen it before (which might involve doing a quick Google search).

To find out whether the string matches the regex, we can use the string **match** method:

```
> s.match(zipCode);
[ '90210',
  index: 14,
  input: 'Beverly Hills 90210 was a \'90s TV show set in Los Angeles. 91125 is
  another ZIP code in the Los Angeles area.' ]
```

The result is the same weird pseudo-array we saw in Section 4.3.1, but at least it gives the same result when run a second time:

---

7. Image courtesy of kitleong/123RF.

Figure 4.7: 91125 is a dedicated ZIP code for the campus of the California Institute of Technology (Caltech).

```
> s.match(zipCode);
[ '90210',
  index: 14,
  input: 'Beverly Hills 90210 was a \'90s TV show set in Los Angeles. 91125 is
  another ZIP code in the Los Angeles area.' ]
```

The **match** method is especially useful in conditionals; recalling the "bang bang" notation from Section 2.4.2, we can evaluate the match in a boolean context:

```
> !!s.match(zipCode);
true
```

Thus, we can do things like this:

```
> if (s.match(zipCode)) {
    "Looks like there's at least one ZIP code in the string!";
  }
'Looks like there\'s at least one ZIP code in the string!'
```

Even better, there's a common technique for matching *all* occurrences of a regular expression using the "global flag" **g** after the second slash:

```
> zipCode = /\d{5}/g;      // Use 'g' to set the 'global' flag.
/\d{5}/g
```

The resulting output is pleasantly intuitive:

```
> s.match(zipCode);
[ '90210', '91125' ]
```

The result here is simply an array of the ZIP codes detected in the string, suitable for joining (Section 3.4.3) or iterating (Section 3.5 and Section 5.4).

Our final example of regexes combines the power of pattern matching with the **split** method we saw in Section 3.1. In that section, we split on spaces, like this:

```
> "ant bat cat duck".split(" ");
[ 'ant', 'bat', 'cat', 'duck' ]
```

We can obtain the same result in a more robust way by splitting on *whitespace*, which consists of spaces, tabs (indicated with **\t**), and newlines (indicated with **\n**).

Consulting the quick reference (Figure 4.5), we find that the regex for whitespace is **\s**, and the way to indicate "one or more" is the plus sign **+**. Thus, we can split on whitespace as follows:

```
> "ant bat cat duck".split(/\s+/);
[ 'ant', 'bat', 'cat', 'duck' ]
```

The reason this is so nice is that now we can get the same result if the strings are separated by multiple spaces, tabs, newlines, etc.:[8]

```
> "ant    bat\tcat\nduck".split(/\s+/);
[ 'ant', 'bat', 'cat', 'duck' ]
```

We also see here the value of the literal constructor: Especially when using short regexes, there's no need to define an intermediate variable; instead, we can use the literal regex directly.

---

8. This pattern is so useful that it's the default behavior for **split** in some languages (notably Ruby), so that **"ant\tbat cat".split** is **["ant", "bat", "cat"]**.

Figure 4.8: ZIP code 10118-0110 (the Empire State Building).

4.3.3 Exercises

1. Write a regex that matches the extended-format ZIP code consisting of five digits, a hyphen, and a four-digit extension (such as 10118-0110). Confirm that it works using **String#match** and the caption in Figure 4.8.[9]

2. Write a regex that splits only on newlines. Such regexes are useful for splitting a block of text into separate lines. In particular, test your regex by pasting the poem in Listing 4.2 into the console and using **sonnet.split(/your regex/)**. What is the length of the resulting array?

Listing 4.2: Some text with newlines.

```
> const sonnet = `Let me not to the marriage of true minds
Admit impediments. Love is not love
Which alters when it alteration finds,
```

---

9. Image courtesy of jordi2r/123RF.

```
Or bends with the remover to remove.
O no, it is an ever-fixed mark
That looks on tempests and is never shaken;
It is the star to every wand'ring bark,
Whose worth's unknown, although his height be taken.
Love's not time's fool, though rosy lips and cheeks
Within his bending sickle's compass come:
Love alters not with his brief hours and weeks,
But bears it out even to the edge of doom.
   If this be error and upon me proved,
   I never writ, nor no man ever loved.`;
```

4.4 Plain Objects

The word *object* is used in various contexts in JavaScript, usually referring to the abstract idea of a collection of data (properties) and functions (methods). As noted in Section 2.4, (almost) everything in JavaScript is an object, and we'll see in Chapter 7 how to define objects that parallel built-in objects like **String**, **Array**, and **RegExp**. In this section, we'll focus on *plain objects*, which are simpler to define than the more general objects we've encountered so far.

In general, objects in JavaScript can be dizzyingly complex, but in their simplest incarnation they work much like hashes (also called *associative arrays*) in other languages. You can think of them as being like regular arrays but with strings rather than integers as indices. Each element is thus a pair of values: a string (the *key*) and an element of any type (the *value*). These elements are also known as *key–value pairs*.

As a simple example, let's create an object to store the first and last names of a user, such as we might have in a web application:

```
> let user = {};                 // {} is an empty Object.
{}
> user["firstName"] = "Michael"; // Key "firstName", value "Michael"
'Michael'
> user["lastName"] = "Hartl";    // Key "lastName", value "Hartl"
'Hartl'
```

As you can see, an empty **Object** is represented by curly braces, and we can assign values using the same square bracket syntax as for arrays. We can retrieve values in the same way:

```
> user["firstName"];        // Element access is like arrays
'Michael'
> user["lastName"];
'Hartl'
```

The keys in our object are nothing other than the *properties* we first met in Section 2.4, and as such they can also be accessed using the dot notation we saw with, e.g., **string.length**:

```
> user.firstName;          // Element access using the dot notation
'Michael'
> user.lastName;
'Hartl'
```

Deciding which syntax to use is a matter of context and style. Note that in either case an undefined key/property name simply returns **undefined**:

```
> user["dude"];
undefined
> user.dude;
undefined
> !!user.dude
false
```

The last line here is a reminder that **undefined** is **false** in a boolean context, which you may recall if you solved the corresponding exercise in Section 3.2.1.

Finally, we can simply display or define the full object, thereby showing the key–value pairs (Listing 4.3).

Listing 4.3: A literal representation of an object.

```
> user;
{ firstName: 'Michael', lastName: 'Hartl' }
> let otherUser = { firstName: 'Foo', lastName: 'Bar' };
> otherUser["firstName"];
'Foo'
> otherUser["lastName"];
'Bar'
```

4.4.1 Exercise

1. Show that **new Object()** also works to create a new empty object. What happens if you give the object constructor an argument equal to the output of Listing 4.3?

4.5 Application: Unique Words

Let's apply plain objects to a challenging exercise, consisting of our longest program so far. Our task is to extract all of the unique words in a fairly long piece of text, and count how many times each word appears.

Because the sequence of commands is rather extensive, our main tool will be a JavaScript file (Section 1.4), executed using the **node** command. (We're not going to make it a self-contained shell script as in Section 1.5 because we don't intend this to be a general-purpose utility program.) At each stage, I suggest using a Node REPL to execute the code interactively if you have any question about the effects of a given command.

Let's start by creating our file:

```
$ touch count.js
```

Now fill it with a **const** containing the text, which we'll choose to be Shakespeare's Sonnet 116[10] (Figure 4.9),[11] as borrowed from Listing 4.2 and shown again in Listing 4.4.

Listing 4.4: Adding some text as a **const**.
count.js

```
const sonnet = `Let me not to the marriage of true minds
Admit impediments. Love is not love
Which alters when it alteration finds,
Or bends with the remover to remove.
O no, it is an ever-fixed mark
That looks on tempests and is never shaken;
It is the star to every wand'ring bark,
Whose worth's unknown, although his height be taken.
```

---

10. Note that in the original pronunciation used in Shakespeare's time, words like "love" and "remove" rhymed, as did "come" and "doom".

11. Image courtesy of psychoshadowmaker/123RF.

```
Love's not time's fool, though rosy lips and cheeks
Within his bending sickle's compass come:
Love alters not with his brief hours and weeks,
But bears it out even to the edge of doom.
    If this be error and upon me proved,
    I never writ, nor no man ever loved.`;
```

Note that Listing 4.4 uses the backtick syntax (Section 2.2.1), which (as it turns out) allows us to break text across lines (unlike regular quotes).[12] *Note*: Because this syntax is relatively new, some text editors (notably some versions of Sublime Text) might need to be configured to highlight it properly.

Next, we'll initialize our object, which we'll call **uniques** because it will have an entry for each unique word in the text:

```
let uniques = {};
```

Figure 4.9: Sonnet 116 compares love's constancy to the guide star for a wandering bark (ship).

---

12. I had to Google around to learn how to do this.

For the purposes of this exercise, we'll define a "word" as a run of one or more *word characters* (i.e., letters or numbers, though there are none of the latter in the present text). This match can be accomplished with a regular expression (Section 4.3), which includes a pattern (\w) for exactly this case (Figure 4.5):

```
let words = sonnet.match(/\w+/g);
```

This uses the "global" **g** flag and the **match** method from Section 4.3.2 to return an array of all the strings that match "one or more word characters in a row". (Extending this pattern to include apostrophes (so that it matches, e.g., "wand'ring" as well) is left as an exercise (Section 4.5.2).)

At this point, the file should look like Listing 4.5.

Listing 4.5: Adding an object and the matching words.
count.js

```
const sonnet = `Let me not to the marriage of true minds
Admit impediments. Love is not love
Which alters when it alteration finds,
Or bends with the remover to remove.
O no, it is an ever-fixed mark
That looks on tempests and is never shaken;
It is the star to every wand'ring bark,
Whose worth's unknown, although his height be taken.
Love's not time's fool, though rosy lips and cheeks
Within his bending sickle's compass come:
Love alters not with his brief hours and weeks,
But bears it out even to the edge of doom.
    If this be error and upon me proved,
    I never writ, nor no man ever loved.`;

let uniques = {};
let words = sonnet.match(/\w+/g);
```

Now for the heart of our program. We're going to loop through the **words** array (Section 3.5) and do the following:

1. If the word already has an entry in the **uniques** object, increment its count by **1**.
2. If the word doesn't have an entry yet in **uniques**, initialize it to **1**.

The result, using the **+=** operator we met briefly in Section 4.3.2, looks like this:

```
for (let i = 0; i < words.length; i++) {
  let word = words[i];
  if (uniques[word]) {
    uniques[word] += 1;
  } else {
    uniques[word] = 1;
  }
}
```

Among other things, we see here the power of the bracket access notation, as there would be no way to accomplish this same task using the dot syntax. Note also that we're relying on **uniques[word]** being undefined (**false** in a boolean context) if **word** isn't yet a valid key.

Finally, we'll print out the result to the terminal:

```
console.log(uniques)
```

The full program (with added comments) appears as in Listing 4.6.

Listing 4.6: A program to count words in text.

count.js

```
const sonnet = `Let me not to the marriage of true minds
Admit impediments. Love is not love
Which alters when it alteration finds,
Or bends with the remover to remove.
O no, it is an ever-fixed mark
That looks on tempests and is never shaken;
It is the star to every wand'ring bark,
Whose worth's unknown, although his height be taken.
Love's not time's fool, though rosy lips and cheeks
Within his bending sickle's compass come:
Love alters not with his brief hours and weeks,
But bears it out even to the edge of doom.
    If this be error and upon me proved,
    I never writ, nor no man ever loved.`;

// Unique words
let uniques = {};
// All words in the text
let words = sonnet.match(/\w+/g);
```

```
// Iterate through `words` and build up an associative array of unique words.
for (let i = 0; i < words.length; i++) {
  let word = words[i];
  if (uniques[word]) {
    uniques[word] += 1;
  } else {
    uniques[word] = 1;
  }
}

console.log(uniques)
```

It's worth noting that, even in a relatively short program like Listing 4.6, it can be tricky to get all the braces, parentheses, etc., to match up. A good text editor can help; for example, when the cursor is next to a closing curly brace, Atom displays subtle bars under each member of the opening/closing pair (Figure 4.10).

The result of running **count.js** in the terminal looks something like this:

```
$ node count.js
{ Let: 1,
  me: 2,
  not: 4,
  to: 4,
  the: 4,
  marriage: 1,
  .
  .
  .
  upon: 1,
  proved: 1,
  I: 1,
  writ: 1,
  nor: 1,
  man: 1,
  loved: 1 }
```

4.5.1 Map

Although native JavaScript objects can be used as hashes/associative arrays (as we've done above), they do have their weaknesses, such as slower performance and limited support for extracting keys and values. JavaScript comes with a dedicated **Map** object to address these limitations, with **set** and **get** methods for setting and getting values using keys:

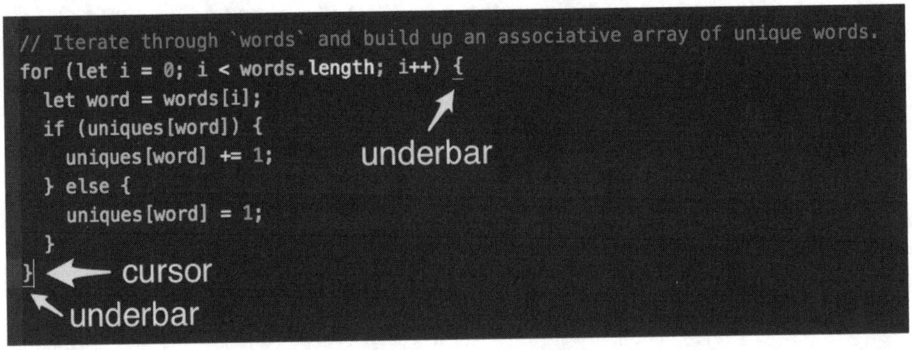

```
// Iterate through `words` and build up an associative array of unique words.
for (let i = 0; i < words.length; i++) {
  let word = words[i];
  if (uniques[word]) {
    uniques[word] += 1;        underbar
  } else {
    uniques[word] = 1;
  }
} ← cursor
  underbar
```

Figure 4.10: Text editors can help immensely in matching up curly braces, etc.

```
> let uniques = new Map();
> uniques.set("loved", 0);
Map { 'loved' => 0 }
> let currentValue = uniques.get("loved");
> uniques.set("loved", currentValue + 1);
Map { 'loved' => 1 }
```

Combining the techniques shown above to rewrite the **count.js** program is left as an exercise (Section 4.5.2).

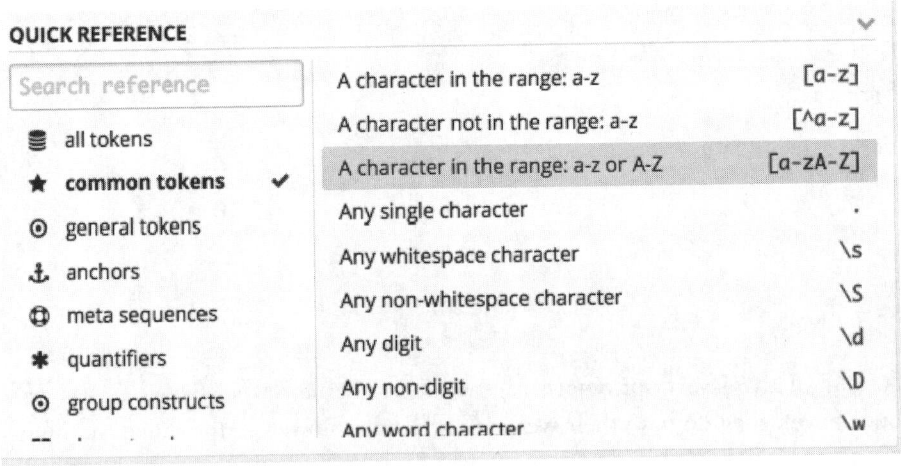

QUICK REFERENCE

Search reference	
🗃 all tokens	A character in the range: a-z	[a-z]
⭐ **common tokens** ✓	A character not in the range: a-z	[^a-z]
◎ general tokens	A character in the range: a-z or A-Z	[a-zA-Z]
⚓ anchors	Any single character	.
⊕ meta sequences	Any whitespace character	\s
✳ quantifiers	Any non-whitespace character	\S
◎ group constructs	Any digit	\d
	Any non-digit	\D
	Any word character	\w

Figure 4.11: An exercise hint.

4.5.2 Exercises

1. Extend the regex used in Listing 4.6 to include an apostrophe, so it matches, e.g., "wand'ring". *Hint*: Combine the first reference regex at regex101 (Figure 4.11) with **\w**, an apostrophe, and the plus operator **+**.

2. Rewrite Listing 4.6 using **Map** (Section 6.1) instead of native JavaScript objects.

CHAPTER 5

Functions

So far in this tutorial, we've repeatedly mentioned JavaScript functions, and in this chapter we'll finally learn how to define functions of our own. The resulting ability gives us greater flexibility as programmers, and enables powerful techniques like **forEach** (Section 5.4) and *functional programming* (Chapter 6). Functions: achievement unlocked (Figure 5.1).

5.1 Function Definitions

As we saw in Section 1.2, function calls in JavaScript consist of a *name* and zero or more arguments enclosed in parentheses:

```
> console.log("hello, world!");
hello, world!
```

As discussed in Section 2.5, functions attached to objects (such as **log** attached to **console**) are also called *methods*.

One of the most important tasks in programming involves defining our own functions. Let's take a look at a simple example in the REPL. We'll define a function called

Figure 5.1: Time to level up.

91

stringMessage that takes a single argument and returns a message based on whether the argument is empty or not:

```
> function stringMessage(string) {
    if (string) {
      return "The string is nonempty.";
    } else {
      return "It's an empty string!";
    }
  }
undefined
```

Note the use of **return** to indicate the *return value* of the function. The result can be seen by calling the function in the REPL:

```
> stringMessage("honey badger");
'The string is nonempty.'
> stringMessage("");
'It\'s an empty string!'
```

It's important to understand that the name of the function argument is irrelevant as far as the caller is concerned. In other words, the first example above could replace **string** with any other valid variable name, such as **asdf**, and it would work just the same:

```
> function stringMessage(asdf) {
    if (asdf) {
      return "The string is nonempty.";
    } else {
      return "It's an empty string!";
    }
  }
undefined
> stringMessage("honey badger");
'The string is nonempty.'
> stringMessage("");
'It\'s an empty string!'
```

5.1.1 Sorting Numerical Arrays

We can apply functions to solve the conundrum encountered in Section 3.4.1, where we saw that JavaScript sorts even numerical arrays "alphabetically" by default:

```
> let a = [8, 17, 42, 99];
> a.sort();
[ 17, 42, 8, 99 ]
```

To sort an array numerically, we can define a function (which we'll call **number-Compare**) that takes in two numbers **a** and **b** and returns **1** when **a > b**, **-1** when **a < b**, and **0** when they're equal. This is the form required by the Array sort documentation (https://developer.mozilla.org/en-US/docs/Web/JavaScript/Reference/Global_Objects/Array/sort), and as we'll see it will let **sort** figure out that we want to sort the array numerically rather than alphabetically. The result appears in Listing 5.1.

Listing 5.1: Comparing numbers numerically.

```
> function numberCompare(a, b) {
    if (a > b) {
      return 1;
    } else if (a < b) {
      return -1;
    } else {
      return 0;
    }
  }
```

We can test this directly as follows:

```
> numberCompare(8, 17);
-1
> numberCompare(17, 99);
-1
> numberCompare(99, 42);
1
> numberCompare(99, 99);
0
```

At this point, we can sort the array by giving **sort** a *function argument*, which causes it to change its default comparison:

```
> a.sort(numberCompare);
[ 8, 17, 42, 99 ]
```

This is the result we're looking for. Under the hood, JavaScript is marching through the array and asking the question, "What is the value of **numberCompare(a, b)**? If it's negative, **a** goes before **b**; if it's positive, **b** goes before **a**. (If they're equal, it doesn't matter.)" The result is an array sorted according to what we intuitively expect.

We'll see an even better way to sort arrays when we learn about *anonymous functions* (functions without a name) in Section 5.4. In particular, an exercise in Section 5.4.1 includes the most idiomatically correct way to sort JavaScript arrays numerically (Listing 5.17).

5.1.2 Fat Arrow

ES6 adds a second method for defining functions known as a "fat arrow", indicated with an equals sign followed by a right angle bracket: **=>**. We can define an alternate string message function by combining **=>** and the **let** keyword:

```
> let altStringMessage = (string) => {
    if (string) {
      return "The string is nonempty.";
    } else {
      return "It's an empty string!";
    }
  }
> altStringMessage("honey badger");
'The string is nonempty '
```

Here **(string)   =>   ...** says to create a function with one argument (**string**) defined by the code to the right of the arrow. In other words,

```
function name(arg) {
  // code
}
```

is the same as

```
let name = (arg) => {
  // code
}
```

Some developers prefer to use this alternate notation for *all* their functions, and this may eventually be a universal practice, but for now the use of **function** is *very* common. It also maps more cleanly to the way you actually call functions:

```
function foo(bar, baz) {
  // do something with bar and baz
}

let x = 1;
let y = 2;
let result = foo(x, y);
```

Because the actual code here uses **foo(x, y)**, it's nice to see a similar sequence of characters appear in the function definition.

In this tutorial, we'll generally stick to using **function** to define functions, but in some contexts we will use the arrow notation for anonymous functions, especially in the context of the *functional programming* techniques discussed in Chapter 6.

As with **var** and **let**/**const**, both **function** and **=>** are in common use. Even if you standardize on one convention for your own code, you have to know both syntaxes in order to read code written by others.

5.1.3 Exercise

1. Using **function**, define a **square** function that returns the square of a number. Do the same with an analogous **altSquare** function using the fat arrow notation.

5.2 Functions in a File

Although defining functions in a REPL is convenient for demonstration purposes, it's a bit cumbersome, and a better practice is to put them in a file (as we did with the script in Section 4.5). We'll start by defining a function directly in the **index.html** file created in Section 1.2, and will then move the function to an even more convenient external file.

Recall from Section 4.2 that **Date** objects have a **getDay()** method that returns the index corresponding to the day of the week (**0** for Sunday, **1** for Monday, etc.). In Listing 4.1, we defined a **const** for the days of the week, and then defined a **dayName** variable using **getDay()**:

```
const daysOfTheWeek = ["Sunday", "Monday", "Tuesday", "Wednesday",
                       "Thursday", "Friday", "Saturday"];
let now = new Date();
```

```
let dayName = daysOfTheWeek[now.getDay()];
alert(`Hello, world! Happy ${dayName}.`);
```

It would be convenient to *encapsulate* this definition and logic in a **dayName**
function, so that we could write our alert like this:

```
alert(`Hello, world! Happy ${dayName(now)}.`);
```

This eliminates the use of the **dayName** variable, instead replacing it with the function
call **dayName(now)**.

Applying the function definition syntax from Section 5.1 leads to the following
dayName function:

```
function dayName(date) {
  const daysOfTheWeek = ["Sunday", "Monday", "Tuesday", "Wednesday",
                         "Thursday", "Friday", "Saturday"];
  return daysOfTheWeek[date.getDay()];
}
```

Note how we've switched from the variable **now** to the more generic-sounding **date**,
which is a way of indicating that our function works with any date that's passed
to it.

Putting this definition into the code from Listing 4.1 nicely separates the **alert**
logic from the code used to generate the day of the week, as shown in Listing 5.2.
The result appears in Figure 5.2.

Listing 5.2: Factoring the day of the week into a function.

index.html

```
<!DOCTYPE html>
<html>
  <head>
    <title>Learn Enough JavaScript</title>
    <meta charset="utf-8">
    <script>
      function dayName(date) {
        const daysOfTheWeek = ["Sunday", "Monday", "Tuesday", "Wednesday",
                               "Thursday", "Friday", "Saturday"];
        return daysOfTheWeek[date.getDay()];
      }

      let now = new Date();
```

```
      alert(`Hello, world! Happy ${dayName(now)}.`);
    </script>
  </head>
  <body>

  </body>
</html>
```

We can make the code in Listing 5.2 even cleaner by factoring the **dayName** function into a separate file and then including it into our page. We'll start by cutting the function and pasting it into a new file, **day.js**:

```
$ touch day.js
```

Figure 5.2: The result of a functional greeting.

The resulting files appear as in Listing 5.3 and Listing 5.4.[1]

Listing 5.3: The **dayName** function in a file.

day.js

```
// Returns the day of the week for the given date.
function dayName(date) {
  const daysOfTheWeek = ["Sunday", "Monday", "Tuesday", "Wednesday",
                         "Thursday", "Friday", "Saturday"];
  return daysOfTheWeek[date.getDay()];
}
```

Listing 5.4: Our greeting with a function in a file.

index.html

```
<!DOCTYPE html>
<html>
  <head>
    <title>Learn Enough JavaScript</title>
    <meta charset="utf-8">
    <script>
      let now = new Date();
      alert(`Hello, world! Happy ${dayName(now)}!`);
    </script>
  </head>
  <body>

  </body>
</html>
```

As you can verify by reloading the browser, at this point our **index.html** page is simply blank—there's no alert, and the JavaScript doesn't work. The default behavior is simply a silent error, but using the browser console (Section 1.3.1) shows the problem, as seen in Figure 5.3. Using the console in this manner is a powerful debugging technique—if your JavaScript ever just silently fails, firing up the browser console should be your strategy of first resort (Box 5.1).[2]

---

1. In some editors, you can use Shift-Command-V to paste in a selection using the local indentation level, which saves us the trouble of dedenting it by hand.

2. @ThePracticalDev image used with permission.

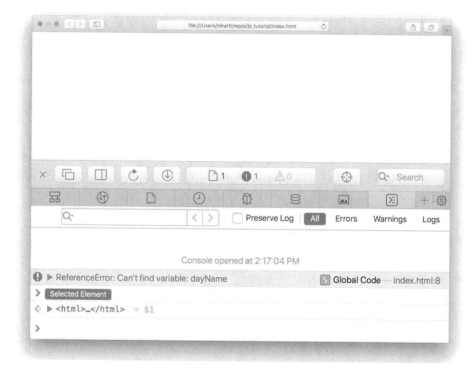

Figure 5.3: Using the browser console to find an error.

Box 5.1: Debugging JavaScript

One skill that's an essential part of technical sophistication is *debugging*: the art of finding and correcting errors in computer programs. While there's no substitute for experience, here are some techniques that should give you a leg up when tracking down the inevitable glitches in your code:

- *Fire up the browser console.* Often, this alone will allow you to identify the bug, especially when the error is silent (i.e., when the program just fails in the browser without any indication of why).

- *Trace the execution with logs or alerts.* When trying to figure out why a particular program is going awry, it's often helpful to display variable values with temporary `console.log` or `alert` statements, which can be removed when the bug is fixed.

- *Comment out code.* It's sometimes a good idea to comment out code you suspect is unrelated to the problem to allow you to focus on the code that isn't working.

- *Use the REPL.* Firing up the REPL and pasting in the problematic code is frequently an excellent way to isolate the problem.

- *Google it.* Googling error messages or other search terms related to the bug (which often leads to helpful threads at Stack Overflow) is an essential skill for every modern software developer (Figure 5.4).

The problem is that we've removed **dayName** from the **script** section of **index.html**, so naturally our page has no idea what it is. The solution is to include it using a second script tag with the **src** (source) attribute pointing to the file containing the definition:

```
<script src="day.js"></script>
<script>
  let now = new Date();
  alert(`Hello, world! Happy ${dayName(now)}!`);
</script>
```

This code might look familiar, since it is similar to the syntax for including images (https://www.learnenough.com/html-tutorial/filling_in_the_index_page #sec-images) (Figure 5.5):[3]

```
<img src="images/kitten.jpg" alt="An adorable kitten">
```

In particular, **src** needs to have the full path to the file, so a JavaScript source file **site.js** in a **scripts/** directory would be referenced using

```
<script src="scripts/site.js"></script>
```

---

3. Image courtesy of halfmax.ru/Shutterstock.

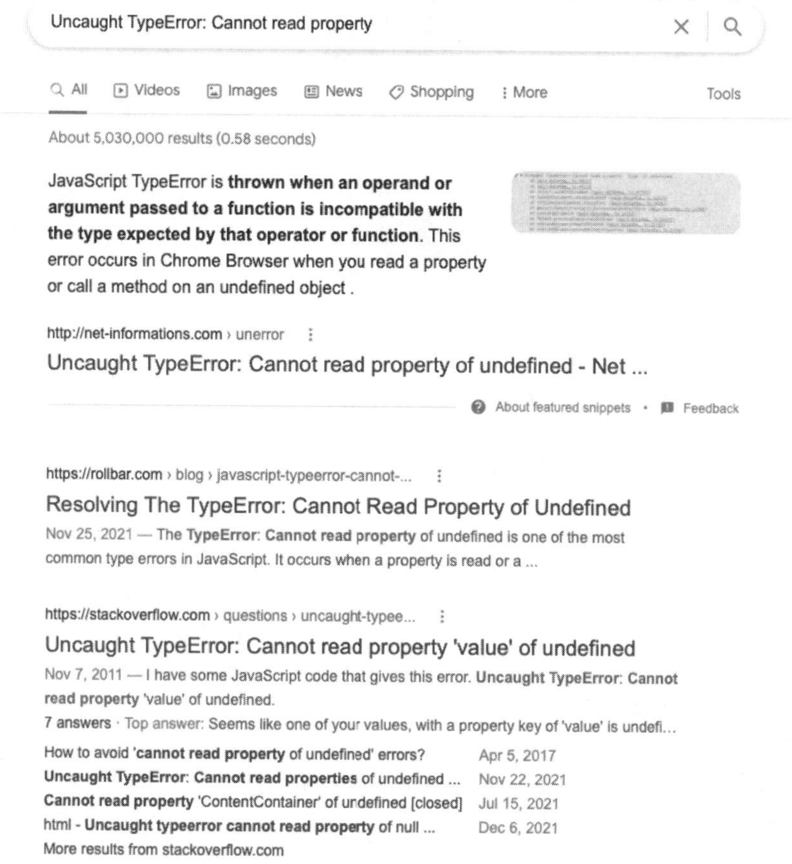

Figure 5.4: How did people ever debug before Google?

The result of putting our new `script` tag with `src` into `index.html` appears in Listing 5.5. Upon reloading the page, our greeting now appears as expected (Figure 5.6).

Figure 5.5: Recognize this cutie from *Learn Enough HTML, CSS and Layout to Be Dangerous?*

Listing 5.5: Using a function from an external file.
index.html

```
<!DOCTYPE html>
<html>
  <head>
    <title>Learn Enough JavaScript</title>
    <meta charset="utf-8">
    <script src="day.js"></script>
    <script>
      let now = new Date();
      alert(`Hello, world! Happy ${dayName(now)}!`);
    </script>
  </head>
  <body>

  </body>
</html>
```

It's important to note that the source script has to come *before* any functions defined in the script are used. Otherwise, the result is the same as in Figure 5.3. Confirming this is left as an exercise (Section 5.2.1).

Figure 5.6: The greeting restored.

5.2.1 Exercises

1. What happens if the **src** line in Listing 5.5 comes after the main script? What is the error in the console?

2. Let's replace the interpolated string in Listing 5.4 with a **greeting** function in **day.js**. Fill in the code in Listing 5.6 to get Listing 5.7 to work.

Listing 5.6: Defining a **greeting** function.
day.js

```
// Returns the day of the week for the given date.
function dayName(date) {
  const daysOfTheWeek = ["Sunday", "Monday", "Tuesday", "Wednesday",
                         "Thursday", "Friday", "Saturday"];
```

```
  return daysOfTheWeek[date.getDay()];
}

// Returns a greeting for the given date.
function greeting(date) {
  // FILL IN
}
```

Listing 5.7: Using the **greeting** function.
index.html

```
<!DOCTYPE html>
<html>
  <head>
    <title>Learn Enough JavaScript</title>
    <meta charset="utf-8">
    <script src="day.js"></script>
    <script>
      let now = new Date();
      alert(greeting(now));
    </script>
  </head>
  <body>

  </body>
</html>
```

5.3 Method Chaining

In this section, we'll start developing the palindrome theme mentioned in the introduction (Chapter 1). Our goal is to write a function called **palindrome** that returns
true if its argument is the same forward and backward, and **false** otherwise.

We can express the simplest possible definition of a palindrome as "a string and
the string reversed are the same." (We'll steadily expand this definition over time.) In
code, we can write this definition as follows:

```
function palindrome(string) {
  return string === reverse(string);
}
```

As required, this will return **true** if a string is a palindrome (equal to its own reverse), and **false** otherwise. There's just one problem, though: JavaScript has no native way to reverse a string, so **reverse(string)** in our proposed implementation won't work. This means we'll have to write the **reverse** function ourselves.

Our technique involves a useful practice called *method chaining*, whereby we call a series of methods one after the other. In particular, although JavaScript doesn't have a native way to reverse strings, we saw in Section 3.4.1 that it *does* have a native way to reverse *arrays*:

```
> let a = [ 17, 42, 8, 99 ];
> a.reverse();
[ 99, 8, 42, 17 ]
```

Meanwhile, we saw in Section 3.1 how to decompose a string into its constituent characters by splitting on the empty string **""**:

```
> "racecar".split("");
[ 'r', 'a', 'c', 'e', 'c', 'a', 'r' ]
```

Finally, we learned in Section 3.4.3 that the **join** method effectively undoes a split:

```
> [ 'r', 'a', 'c', 'e', 'c', 'a', 'r' ].join("");
'racecar'
```

This discussion suggests the following algorithm for writing a **reverse** method:

1. Split a string on the empty string to create an array of characters.
2. Reverse the array.
3. Join the array on the empty string to create the reversed string.

Because of method chaining, we can implement this algorithm in a single line:

```
> let string = "Racecar";
> string.split("").reverse().join("")
'racecaR'
```

(Because of the way **split("")** works, this method will actually fail for text containing more complex characters like emojis. We'll fix this minor blemish in Section 5.3.1.)

Let's put the **reverse** function into a library for detecting palindromes, which we'll call **palindrome.js**:

```
$ touch palindrome.js
```

The resulting function appears in Listing 5.8.

Listing 5.8: A function for reversing a string.
palindrome.js

```
// Reverses a string.
function reverse(string) {
  return string.split("").reverse().join("");
}
```

Note that Listing 5.8 includes a *documentation comment* (introduced briefly in Listing 5.3) explaining the purpose of the function. This isn't strictly required, but it's an excellent practice for the sake of future programmers (including us!).

To check the effect of Listing 5.8, we can **load** the external file in a Node REPL using "dot load" (note the lack of an ending semicolon, which is necessary to avoid an error):

```
> .load palindrome.js
> reverse("Racecar");
'racecaR'
```

(Using **.load** simply runs every line of the file inside the REPL. This has the side effect of altering our command history, so that using "up arrow" to retrieve previous commands is less useful than it would be otherwise. There's really no way around this; unfortunately, as a consequence of its web-browser origins, JavaScript doesn't have a native way to include one file into another, so the **.load** kluge is the best we can do.)

We are now in a position to write the first version of our palindrome function, which will compare a string to its own reverse:

```
> string;      // Just a reminder of what our string is
'Racecar'
> string === reverse(string);
false
```

The resulting definition of **palindrome** appears in Listing 5.9.

Listing 5.9: Our initial **palindrome** function.
palindrome.js

```
// Reverses a string.
function reverse(string) {
  return string.split("").reverse().join("");
}

// Returns true for a palindrome, false otherwise.
function palindrome(string) {
  return string === reverse(string);
}
```

Reloading **palindrome.js** lets us check the effect of the **palindrome** function directly:

```
> .load palindrome.js
> palindrome("To be or not to be");
false
> palindrome("Racecar");
false
> palindrome("level");
true
```

It works!

There's one minor refinement it would be nice to add right away, which is the ability to detect palindromes independent of case. In other words, we'd like to return **true** for something like "Racecar", even though the initial "R" is capitalized. We can do this by converting the string to lowercase before making the comparison, which we can do using the **toLowerCase** method from Section 2.5:

```
> let processedContent = string.toLowerCase();
> processedContent;
'racecar'
> processedContent === reverse(processedContent);
true
```

Putting this into **palindrome.js** gives Listing 5.10.

Listing 5.10: Detecting palindromes independent of case.

palindrome.js

```
// Reverses a string.
function reverse(string) {
  return string.split("").reverse().join("");
}

// Returns true for a palindrome, false otherwise.
function palindrome(string) {
  let processedContent = string.toLowerCase();
  return processedContent === reverse(processedContent);
}
```

Using the REPL, we can confirm that it worked:

```
> .load palindrome.js
> palindrome("racecar");
true
> palindrome("Racecar");
true
> palindrome("Able was I ere I saw Elba");
true
```

5.3.1 Caveat Emoji

There's one minor caveat to the **reverse** method developed in Listing 5.10, which is that it won't quite work with text that includes more complicated characters like emojis. For example, attempting to reverse a sentence containing the "fox face" and "dog face" emojis yields a garbled result, as shown in Figure 5.7.

Figure 5.7: A failed emoji reversal.

The reason for this is that each emoji is effectively represented as two separate characters, and splitting on the empty string as in Listing 5.10 splits each emoji in half (ouch!). The solution is to create an array from a string in a different way, using a custom array method called **Array.from()**:

```
> Array.from('honey badger');
[ 'h', 'o', 'n', 'e', 'y', ' ', 'b', 'a', 'd', 'g', 'e', 'r' ]
```

Replacing **split** in Listing 5.10 with this improved method gives the updated **reverse** code in Listing 5.11.

Listing 5.11: Improving **reverse** using **Array.from**.

```
// Reverses a string.
function reverse(string) {
  return Array.from(string).reverse().join("")
}

// Returns true for a palindrome, false otherwise.
function palindrome(string) {
  let processedContent = string.toLowerCase();
  return processedContent === reverse(processedContent);
}
```

Confirming that this code works is left as an exercise.

5.3.2   Exercises

1. Using method chaining and the template in Listing 5.12, write a function **emailParts** to return an array of the username and domain for a standard email address of the form **username@example.com**. *Note*: Make sure your function returns the same result for **USERNAME@EXAMPLE.COM**.

2. Using the Node REPL, confirm that the **reverse** function defined in Listing 5.11 correctly reverses a string containing emojis. (You may find Emojipedia (https://emojipedia.org/) links to the fox face and dog face emojis helpful.) Your result should look something like Figure 5.8.

Figure 5.8: A successful emoji reversal.

Listing 5.12: Returning the parts of an email.

```
> function emailParts(email) {
    // FILL IN
  }
```

5.4 Iteration for Each

So far, we've seen several examples of *iteration*: for strings (Section 2.6), arrays (Section 3.5), and objects (Section 4.5)—all based on the **for** loop. In this section, we'll learn how to use **forEach** loops, which iterate through each element in an array, without the inconvenience of an auxiliary index variable.

Doing an operation "for each" element in an array means we can change from this:

```
for (let i = 0; i < array.length; i++) {
  console.log(array[i]);
}
```

to this:

```
array.forEach(function(element) {
  console.log(element);
});
```

The latter code allows us to perform actions on each array element directly, without having to access it using **array[i]**.

You can see why we had to wait until now: **forEach** requires that we use a function—in particular, a nameless, or *anonymous*, function—to create a variable for each element in the array.[4] That said, I find it helps not to pronounce "function" (whether aloud or in your head), so that it sounds like "array: for each element <do something>."

To get a better understanding of **forEach**, let's look at a concrete example in the REPL:

```
> [42, 17, 85].forEach(function(element) {
    console.log(element);
  });
42
17
85
```

What's going on here is that **forEach** itself takes a function as an argument, which then returns each element of the corresponding array in turn. The syntax might look a little strange, but this pattern of passing a function to a method is a common one, and you'll soon become accustomed to it. Don't worry too much about exactly what's going on under the hood—instead, focus on the concrete effects.

Using our newfound **forEach** powers, we can rewrite each of the previously encountered **for** loops using **forEach**, starting with the array iteration from Listing 3.4. For convenience, we'll put the code in a file and execute it at the command line:

```
$ touch foreach.js
```

To perform the iteration, all we need is a **forEach** loop whose contents print the element itself instead of printing **a[i]**. The result is shown in Listing 5.13.

Listing 5.13: Iterating through an array with a **forEach** loop.
foreach.js

```
let a = ["ant", "bat", "cat", 42];
a.forEach(function(element) {
  console.log(element);
});
```

---

4. A function (whether named or anonymous) with data attached in this manner is known as a *closure*.

Executing the program in Listing 5.13 at the command line results in the same output we saw in Listing 3.4, as shown in Listing 5.14.

Listing 5.14: The output of an array iteration.

```
$ node foreach.js
ant
cat
bat
42
```

Now let's use **forEach** to rewrite the string iteration from Listing 2.18. Our technique will be to create an array from the string, and then use **forEach** to iterate one element at a time. For the first step, we'll be creating an array from the string using the **Array.from** method introduced at the end of Section 5.3 (Listing 5.11):

```
> Array.from("honey badger");
[ 'h', 'o', 'n', 'e', 'y', ' ', 'b', 'a', 'd', 'g', 'e', 'r' ]
```

The result is an array of characters, which we can then iterate through using **forEach**.

We'll start by including the **soliloquy** variable from Listing 2.15 in the **foreach.js** file, and then use **Array.from** and **forEach**. The resulting code (which we'll place after the array iteration from Listing 5.13) appears as in Listing 5.15.

Listing 5.15: Using a **forEach** loop to iterate through a string.
foreach.js

```
.
.
.
let soliloquy = "To be, or not to be, that is the question:";
Array.from(soliloquy).forEach(function(character) {
  console.log(character);
});
```

Executing the program in Listing 5.15 at the command line results in the same output we saw in Listing 2.18 (preceded in this case by the output from Listing 5.14), as shown in Listing 5.16.

Figure 5.9: Using `forEach` has made Mike Vanier a little happier.

Listing 5.16: The output of a string iteration.

```
$ node foreach.js
ant
bat
cat
42
T
o

b
e
.

.

.
t
i
o
n
:
```

Using the **forEach** method, we can iterate directly through the elements in an array, thereby avoiding having to type out Mike Vanier's *bête noire*, "for (i = 0; i < N; i++)". The result is cleaner code and a happier programmer (Figure 5.9).

5.4.1   Exercises

1. Rewrite the **forEach** loop in Listing 5.13 using the fat arrow notation from Section 5.1.2.

2. We saw in Listing 5.1 how to define a number comparison function that let us sort JavaScript arrays numerically. There we used return values of **1**, **-1**, and **0**, but it turns out **sort** only cares about the *sign* of the comparison, so **17** is the same as **1**, **-42** is the same as **-1**, etc. For numbers **a** and **b**, the value **a - b** has the right sign, so show that the code in Listing 5.17, which uses an anonymous function, correctly sorts the array.

3. Write a **forEach** loop to print the values of the previous exercise.

Listing 5.17: Sorting an array the anonymous way.

```
> let a = [8, 17, 42, 99];
> a.sort(function(a, b) { return a - b; });
[ 8, 17, 42, 99 ]
```

CHAPTER 6

Functional Programming

Having learned how to define functions and apply them in a couple of different contexts, now we're going to take our programming to the next level by learning the basics of *functional programming*, a style of programming that emphasizes—you guessed it—functions. This is a challenging chapter, and you may have to get in some reps to fully grok it (Box 6.1), but the rewards are rich indeed.

Box 6.1: Getting in Your Reps

In contexts ranging from martial arts to chess to language learning, practitioners will reach a point where no amount of analysis or reflection will help them improve—they just need to get in some more repetitions, or "reps".

It's amazing how much you can improve by trying something, kinda-sorta (but maybe not quite) getting it, and then just *doing it again*. In the context of a tutorial like this one, sometimes that means rereading a particularly tricky section or chapter. Some people (including yours truly) will even reread an entire book.

One important aspect of getting in your reps is *suspending self-judgment*—allow yourself not to be good right away. (Many people—including, again, yours truly—often require practice to get good at being okay with not being good right away. Meta-reps, as it were.)

Give yourself a break, get in your reps, and watch your technical sophistication grow by the day.

Functional programming de-emphasizes things like mutation and side effects, focusing instead on applying functions to manipulate and transform arguments to

Figure 6.1: A triumvirate of functional methods.

functions. This definition is rather abstract, and the subject itself is vast, so we'll make things concrete and manageable by focusing on a classic triumvirate of methods commonly used in functional programming: `map`, `filter`, and `reduce` (Figure 6.1).[1]

In each case, our technique will be to perform a task involving a `forEach` loop and a sequence of commands (called "imperative programming",[2] which is what we've mostly been doing so far), and then show how to do the same thing using functional programming.

For convenience, we'll create a file for our explorations, rather than typing everything at the REPL:

```
$ touch functional.js
```

6.1 Map

The first of our triumvirate is the **map** function (Figure 6.2),[3] which lets us map a function over an array of elements. It's often a powerful alternative to looping.

---

1. Images courtesy of Kamira/Shutterstock (left), World History Archive/Alamy Stock Photo (center), and colaimages/Alamy Stock Photo (right).

2. Such programs are written as a series of commands; thus, "imperative," from Latin *imperātīvus*, "proceeding from a command."

3. Image courtesy of Kamira/Shutterstock. The overbars in *Gāius Iūlius Caesar* and other Latin words are *macrons*, which indicate long vowels.

Figure 6.2: The first triumvir, Gāius Iūlius Caesar (Julius Caesar).

For example, suppose we had an array of mixed-case strings, and we wanted to create a corresponding array of lowercase strings joined on a hyphen (making the result appropriate for use in URLs), like this:

```
"North Dakota" -> "north-dakota"
```

Using previous techniques from this tutorial, we could do this as follows:

1. Define a variable containing an array of strings.

2. Define a second variable (initially empty) for the URL-friendly array of strings.

3. For each item in the first array, **push** (Section 3.4.2) a lowercase version (Section 2.5) that's been split on whitespace (Section 4.3.2) and then joined (Section 3.4.3) on hyphens. (You could split on a single space **" "** instead, but splitting on whitespace is so much more robust that it's a good practice to use it by default.)

The result appears in Listing 6.1.

Listing 6.1: Making URL-appropriate strings from an array.

functional.js

```
let states = ["Kansas", "Nebraska", "North Dakota", "South Dakota"];

// urls: Imperative version
function imperativeUrls(elements) {
  let urls = [];
  elements.forEach(function(element) {
    urls.push(element.toLowerCase().split(/\s+/).join("-"));
  });
  return urls;
}
console.log(imperativeUrls(states));
```

This is fairly complicated code, so being able to read Listing 6.1 is a good test of your growing technical sophistication. (If it isn't easy to read, firing up a Node REPL and running it interactively is a good idea.)

The result of running Listing 6.1 looks like this:

```
$ node functional.js
[ 'kansas', 'nebraska', 'north-dakota', 'south-dakota' ]
```

Now let's see how we can do the same thing using **map**, which operates by applying the same function to every element in an array. For example, to square every element in an array of numbers, we can map the function **n * n** over the array, as seen here in the REPL:

```
> [1, 2, 3, 4].map(function(n) { return n * n; });
[ 1, 4, 9, 16 ]
```

Here we've mapped an anonymous function (Section 5.4) over the array, yielding the square of each element. It looks even cleaner in terms of the fat arrow notation (Section 5.1.2):

```
> [1, 2, 3, 4].map( (n) => { return n * n; });
[ 1, 4, 9, 16 ]
```

Even better, for the very common case of a function of a single argument, JavaScript allows us to omit the parentheses, curly braces, and even the **return** keyword, leading to the following incredibly compact code:

```
> [1, 2, 3, 4].map(n => n * n);
[ 1, 4, 9, 16 ]
```

Returning to our main example, we can think of the transformation "lowercase then split then join" as a single operation, and use **map** to apply that operation in sequence to each element in the array. The result is so compact that it easily fits in the REPL:

```
> let states = ["Kansas", "Nebraska", "North Dakota", "South Dakota"];
> states.map(state => state.toLowerCase().split(/\s+/).join('-'));
[ 'kansas', 'nebraska', 'north-dakota', 'south-dakota' ]
```

Pasting into **function.js**, we see just how much shorter it is, as shown in Listing 6.2.

Listing 6.2: Adding a functional technique using **map**.
functional.js

```
let states = ["Kansas", "Nebraska", "North Dakota", "South Dakota"];

// urls: Imperative version
function imperativeUrls(elements) {
  let urls = [];
  elements.forEach(function(element) {
    urls.push(element.toLowerCase().split(/\s+/).join("-"));
  });
  return urls;
}
console.log(imperativeUrls(states));

// urls: Functional version
function functionalUrls(elements) {
  return elements.map(element => element.toLowerCase().split(/\s+/).join('-'));
}
console.log(functionalUrls(states));
```

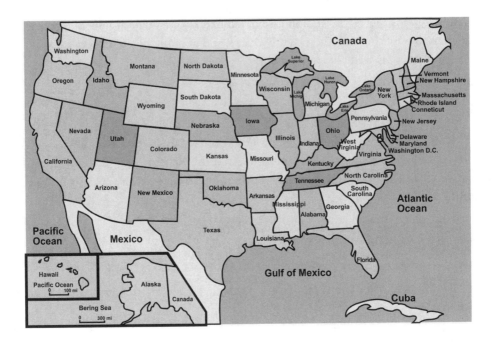

Figure 6.3: Putting some states on the **map**.

We can confirm at the command line that the results are the same:

```
$ node functional.js
[ 'kansas', 'nebraska', 'north-dakota', 'south-dakota' ]
[ 'kansas', 'nebraska', 'north-dakota', 'south-dakota' ]
```

Our functional program has really put the **map** on those states (Figure 6.3).[4]

As a final refinement, let's factor the method chain responsible for making the strings URL-compatible into a separate auxiliary function called **urlify**:

```
// Returns a URL-friendly version of a string.
//  Example: "North Dakota" -> "north-dakota"
function urlify(string) {
  return string.toLowerCase().split(/\s+/).join('-');
}
```

4. Image courtesy of Creative Jen Designs/Shutterstock.

Defining this function in **functional.js** and using it in the imperative and functional versions gives the code in Listing 6.3.

Listing 6.3: Defining an auxiliary function.

functional.js

```js
let states = ["Kansas", "Nebraska", "North Dakota", "South Dakota"];

// Returns a URL-friendly version of a string.
//    Example: "North Dakota" -> "north-dakota"
function urlify(string) {
  return string.toLowerCase().split(/\s+/).join("-");
}

// urls: Imperative version
function imperativeUrls(elements) {
  let urls = [];
  elements.forEach(function(element) {
    urls.push(urlify(element));
  });
  return urls;
}
console.log(imperativeUrls(states));

// urls: Functional version
function functionalUrls(elements) {
  return elements.map(element => urlify(element));
}
console.log(functionalUrls(states));
```

As before, the results are the same:

```
$ node functional.js
[ 'kansas', 'nebraska', 'north-dakota', 'south-dakota' ]
[ 'kansas', 'nebraska', 'north-dakota', 'south-dakota' ]
```

Compared to the imperative version, the functional version is a fifth as many lines (1 instead of 5), doesn't mutate any variables (often an error-prone step in imperative programming), and indeed eliminates the intermediate array (**urls**) entirely. This is the sort of thing that makes Mike Vanier very happy (Figure 6.4).[5]

---

5. Last I checked, Mike's favorite language was a "purely functional" language called Haskell.

Figure 6.4: Functional programming makes Mike Vanier happiest of all.

6.1.1 Exercise

1. Using **map**, write a function that takes in the **states** variable and returns an array of URLs of the form **https://example.com/<urlified form>**.

6.2 Filter

Our second triumvir is **filter** (Figure 6.5),[6] which allows us to filter our data based on some boolean criterion.

Suppose, for example, we wanted to start with the same **states** array defined in Section 6.1 and return a new array consisting of the strings that have only one word. This is exactly the kind of task that **filter** is good for, but as in Section 6.1 we'll write an imperative version first. The steps are fairly straightforward:

1. Define an array to store single-word strings.
2. For each element in the list, **push** it to the storage array if splitting it on whitespace yields an array with length 1.

---

6. Image courtesy of World History Archive/Alamy Stock Photo.

Figure 6.5: The second triumvir, Marcus Licinius Crassus (at one point the richest man in Rome).

The result looks like Listing 6.4.

Listing 6.4: Solving a filtering problem imperatively.

functional.js

```
let states = ["Kansas", "Nebraska", "North Dakota", "South Dakota"];
.
.
.
// singles: Imperative version
function imperativeSingles(elements) {
  let singles = [];
  elements.forEach(function(element) {
    if (element.split(/\s+/).length === 1) {
      singles.push(element);
    }
  });
  return singles;
}
console.log(imperativeSingles(states));
```

Note in Listing 6.4 the familiar pattern from Listing 6.1: First define an auxiliary variable in order to maintain state (no pun intended); then loop over the original array, mutating the variable as necessary; then return the mutated result. It's not particularly pretty, but it works:

```
$ node functional.js
[ 'kansas', 'nebraska', 'north-dakota', 'south-dakota' ]
[ 'kansas', 'nebraska', 'north-dakota', 'south-dakota' ]
[ 'Kansas', 'Nebraska' ]
```

Now let's see how to do the same task using **filter**. As in Section 6.1, we'll start with a simple numerical example in the REPL.

We'll begin by looking at the *modulo operator* **%**, which returns the remainder after dividing an integer by another integer. In other words, **17 % 5** (read "seventeen mod five") is **2**, because 5 goes into 17 three times (giving 15), with a remainder of $17 - 15 = 2$. In particular, considering integers modulo 2 divides them into two *equivalence classes*: even numbers (remainder 0 (mod 2)) and odd numbers (remainder 1 (mod 2)). In code:

```
> 16 % 2;  // even
0
> 17 % 2;  // odd
1
> 16 % 2 === 0;  // even
true
> 17 % 2 === 0;  // odd
false
```

We can combine **%** and **filter** to process an array of numbers and select just the even ones:

```
> [1, 2, 3, 4, 5, 6, 7, 8].filter(n => n % 2 === 0);
[ 2, 4, 6, 8 ]
```

The syntax is almost exactly the same as **map**: We give **filter** a variable (**n**) and then perform a *test* that returns **true** or **false**.

Using this idea, we see that the functional version of Listing 6.4 is much cleaner—indeed, as with **map**, the **filter** version is a single line (a common occurrence in functional programming), as we can see in the REPL:

```
> states.filter(state => state.split(/\s+/).length === 1);
```

Placing the result in our example file again underscores how much more compact the functional version is (Listing 6.5).

Listing 6.5: Solving a filtering problem functionally.

functional.js

```
let states = ["Kansas", "Nebraska", "North Dakota", "South Dakota"];
.
.
.
// singles: Imperative version
function imperativeSingles(elements) {
  let singles = [];
  elements.forEach(function(element) {
    if (element.split(/\s+/).length === 1) {
      singles.push(element);
    }
  });
  return singles;
}
console.log(imperativeSingles(states));

// singles: Functional version
function functionalSingles(elements) {
  return elements.filter(element => element.split(/\s+/).length === 1);
}
console.log(functionalSingles(states));
```

As required, the result is the same:

```
$ node functional.js
[ 'kansas', 'nebraska', 'north-dakota', 'south-dakota' ]
[ 'kansas', 'nebraska', 'north-dakota', 'south-dakota' ]
[ 'Kansas', 'Nebraska' ]
[ 'Kansas', 'Nebraska' ]
```

6.2.1 Exercise

1. Write two **filter** functions that return the Dakotas: one using **String#includes** (Section 2.5) to test for the presence of the string "Dakota" and one using a regex that tests for the length of the split array being **2**.

6.3 Reduce

We reach finally the third member of our triumvirate, the mighty **reduce** (Figure 6.6)[7]—by far the most complicated of the three.

Because **reduce** is particularly challenging, we'll cover two examples. First, we'll make iterative and functional versions of a **sum** operation on arrays of integers. Second, we'll make a plain JavaScript object (Section 4.4) that maps state names to the length of each name, with a result that will look like this:

```
{ "Kansas": 6,
  "Nebraska": 8,
        .
        .
        .
}
```

6.3.1 Reduce, Example 1

We'll begin with an imperative solution for the **sum** function, which involves (as usual) a **forEach** loop and an auxiliary variable (**total**), which we use to accumulate the result. The result appears in Listing 6.6.

Figure 6.6: The third triumvir, Gnaeus Pompēius Magnus (Pompey the Great).

---

7. Image courtesy of colaimages/Alamy Stock Photo.

Listing 6.6: An imperative solution for summing integers.
functional.js

```
.
.
.
let numbers = [1, 2, 3, 4, 5, 6, 7, 8, 9, 10];

// sum: Imperative solution
function imperativeSum(elements) {
  let total = 0;
  elements.forEach(function(n) {
    total += n;
  });
  return total;
}
console.log(imperativeSum(numbers));
```

Again we see the familiar pattern: Initialize an auxiliary variable (**total**) and then loop through the collection, accumulating the result by adding each number to the total.

The result is 55 as required:

```
$ node functional.js
[ 'kansas', 'nebraska', 'north-dakota', 'south-dakota' ]
[ 'kansas', 'nebraska', 'north-dakota', 'south-dakota' ]
[ 'Kansas', 'Nebraska' ]
[ 'Kansas', 'Nebraska' ]
55
```

Now for the **reduce** solution. It's a bit tricky, so let's work in the REPL:

```
> let numbers = [1, 2, 3, 4, 5, 6, 7, 8, 9, 10];
> numbers.reduce((total, n) => {
    total += n;
    return total;
  }, 0);
55
```

You can see what I meant by "tricky". The **reduce** method takes a function of *two* arguments, the first of which is an *accumulator* for the result, and the second of which is the array element itself. The return value of the (anonymous) function gets passed back to **reduce** as the starting value for the next element in the array. The second argument to **reduce** is the initial value of the accumulator (in this case, **0**).

There are two refinements we can make. First, the **+=** operator returns its value, so we can actually increment a value while simultaneously assigning it (or returning it):

```
> let i = 0;
> let j = i += 1;
> i
1
> j
1
```

This means we can return **total += n** directly:

```
> numbers.reduce((total, n) => { return total += n }, 0);
55
```

Second, the initial value is the first element of the array by default (with the **reduce** procedure then starting with the second element), so in this case it can be left off:

```
> numbers.reduce((total, n) => { return total += n });
55
```

Putting the result into our example file shows, as usual, a marked improvement over the iterative version (Listing 6.7).

Listing 6.7: A functional solution for summing integers.

functional.js

```
.
.
.
let numbers = [1, 2, 3, 4, 5, 6, 7, 8, 9, 10];

// sum: Imperative solution
function imperativeSum(elements) {
  let total = 0;
  elements.forEach(function(n) {
    total += n;
  });
  return total;
}
```

```
console.log(imperativeSum(numbers));

// sum: Functional solution
function functionalSum(elements) {
  return elements.reduce((total, n) => return total += n; );
}
console.log(functionalSum(numbers));
```

The result of the functional sum should be the same as for the imperative version:

```
$ node functional.js
[ 'kansas', 'nebraska', 'north-dakota', 'south-dakota' ]
[ 'kansas', 'nebraska', 'north-dakota', 'south-dakota' ]
[ 'Kansas', 'Nebraska' ]
[ 'Kansas', 'Nebraska' ]
55
55
```

Listing 6.7 gives us a hint about the meaning of **reduce**: It's a function that takes the elements of an array and processes (*reduces*) them based on some operation (in this case, addition). This is not always the case, though, and as we'll see in a moment it's often more helpful to think of **reduce** as *accumulating* results and storing them in its first argument (**total** in Listing 6.7).[8]

6.3.2 Reduce, Example 2

To help reinforce **reduce**, let's take a look at a second example. As mentioned above, our task is to make a plain object (associative array) with keys equal to the state names and values equal to their lengths (which could be useful for calculating, e.g., a histogram of word frequencies in a longer document). We can solve this imperatively by initializing a **lengths** object and then iterating through the states, setting **lengths[state]** equal to the corresponding length:

```
lengths[state] = state.length;
```

---

8. For this reason, **reduce** is sometimes called **accumulate** in other languages. See, e.g., "Sequence Operations" (https://mitpress.mit.edu/sites/default/files/sicp/full-text/book/book-Z-H-15.html) in Chapter 2 (https://mitpress.mit.edu/sites/default/files/sicp/full-text/book/book-Z-H-13.html) of *Structure and Interpretation of Computer Programs* (https://mitpress.mit.edu/sites/default/files/sicp/full-text/book/book.html).

The full example appears in Listing 6.8.

Listing 6.8: An imperative solution for state/length correspondence.
functional.js

```
.
.
.
// lengths: Imperative solution
function imperativeLengths(elements) {
  let lengths = {};
  elements.forEach(function(element) {
    lengths[element] = element.length;
  });
  return lengths;
}
console.log(imperativeLengths(states));
```

If we run the program at the command line, the desired associative array appears as the final part of the output:

```
$ node functional.js
.
.
.
{ Kansas: 6, Nebraska: 8, 'North Dakota': 12, 'South Dakota': 12 }
```

The functional solution using **reduce** is trickier. As with the imperative solution, we have a plain **lengths** object, but instead of being an auxiliary variable, it's a parameter to the function:

```
(lengths, state) => {
  lengths[state] = state.length;
  return lengths;
}
```

Meanwhile, the initial value of the **reduce** method, instead of being **0**, is the empty object **{}**:

```
reduce((lengths, state) => {
  lengths[state] = state.length;
  return lengths;
}, {});
```

Note that these are code snippets, not REPL sessions; one disadvantage of **reduce** (and functional solutions generally) is that they are harder to build up incrementally. More on this in a moment.

Taking the above ideas together, we can use **reduce** to march through the **states** array, accumulating the desired associative array in the **lengths** parameter and then returning it, as shown in Listing 6.9.

Listing 6.9: A functional solution for state/length correspondence.

functional.js

```
.
.
.
// lengths: Imperative solution
function imperativeLengths(elements) {
  let lengths = {};
  elements.forEach(function(element) {
    lengths[element] = element.length;
  });
  return lengths;
}
console.log(imperativeLengths(states));

// lengths: Functional solution
function functionalLengths(elements) {
  return elements.reduce((lengths, element) => {
                         lengths[element] = element.length;
                         return lengths;
                      }, {});
}
console.log(functionalLengths(states));
```

Although it is broken across multiple lines in the text editor, the functional solution in Listing 6.9 **return**s the result of a single **reduce**, in close analogy with the functional solutions for **map** (Listing 6.2) and **filter** (Listing 6.5).

As required, the result is the same as the imperative solution:

```
$ node functional.js
.
.
.
{ Kansas: 6, Nebraska: 8, 'North Dakota': 12, 'South Dakota': 12 }
{ Kansas: 6, Nebraska: 8, 'North Dakota': 12, 'South Dakota': 12 }
```

Comparing the imperative and functional solutions in Listing 6.9, the advantages of **reduce** are not as clear as they were in the case of `map` and `filter`. Indeed, a good argument can be made that the imperative solution is clearer.

Which method to use is a matter of taste. I've found that the more you program functionally, the more you want to do it, and there's a strange sort of pleasure in using **reduce** to solve a problem in a single (logical) line. It's also worth noting that **reduce** is a common technique among more advanced programmers, and among other things plays a key role in an important technique (called MapReduce) for dealing efficiently with large datasets.

6.3.3 Functional Programming and TDD

One of the things you may have noticed when building up Listing 6.9 is that the functional solution is harder to break down into steps. The advantage is that we can often condense a functional solution into a single line, but the cost is that it can be harder to understand incrementally. Indeed, I find this to be a consistent pattern across all three functions in our triumvirate; the final destination is often beautifully succinct, but getting there can be a challenge.

My favorite technique for managing this challenge is *test-driven development* (TDD), which involves writing an *automated test* that captures the desired behavior in code. We can then get the test to pass using any method we want, including an ugly but easy-to-understand iterative solution. At that point, we can *refactor* the code—changing its form but not its function—to use a more concise functional solution. As long as the test still passes, we can be confident that the code still works.

In Chapter 8, we'll apply this exact technique to the principal object developed in Chapter 7. In particular, we'll use TDD to implement a fancy extension to the **palindrome** function first seen in Section 5.3, one that detects such complicated palindromes as "A man, a plan, a canal—Panama!" (Figure 6.7).[9]

9. Image courtesy of Everett Collection Historical/Alamy Stock Photo.

Figure 6.7: Teddy Roosevelt was a man with a plan.

6.3.4 Exercises

1. Using **reduce**, write a function that returns the product of all the elements in an array. *Hint*: Where **+=** adds, ***=** multiplies.

2. Remove the newlines in the **reduce** solution from Listing 6.9 to turn it into a single long line. Does it still give the right answer? How long is the resulting line of code?

CHAPTER 7
Objects and Prototypes

In Section 4.4, we learned how to make plain objects, which we used as simple associative arrays of key–value pairs. In this chapter, we'll make more general versions of JavaScript objects, ones that have both properties (data) and methods (functions) attached to them.

7.1 Defining Objects

There is a dizzying variety of ways to define objects in JavaScript, but we'll focus on one of the most classic ways, which is to use functions (Chapter 5). The result will be an object *constructor function* that can be used to create (or *instantiate*) a new object (called an *instance*) using the **new** syntax we first saw in Section 4.2.

We'll start by defining a **Phrase** object. Eventually, we'll use **Phrase** to represent a phrase like "Madam, I'm Adam." that can qualify as a palindrome even if it's not technically the same forward and backward. At first, though, all we'll do is define a **Phrase** constructor function that takes in an argument (the **content**) and sets the property **content**. We'll put this in a file in a moment, but for now let's work in the REPL:

```
> function Phrase(content) {
    this.content = content;
  }
```

Inside the **Phrase** function, **this** represents the object itself, and we can assign it a property just as we did with plain objects in Section 4.4.

The effect of defining **Phrase** is that we can create a new phrase using **new Phrase**:

```
> let greeting = new Phrase("Hello, world!");
```

As with, e.g., the **length** property of **String** objects (Section 2.4), we can access a phrase's content using the familiar dot notation:

```
> greeting.content;
'Hello, world!'
```

Note that object names are conventionally written in CamelCase (Figure 2.3) with a leading capital letter (unlike variables, which start with a lowercase letter). All of the native objects we've seen so far—including **String**, **Array**, **Date**, and **RegExp**—follow this consistent naming convention.

Because we'll be building up to a **Phrase** object that can detect palindromes, we'll work in the **palindrome.js** file we created in Section 5.3. For reference, the file contents are repeated below, along with our simple **Phrase** object definition (Listing 7.1). Note that Listing 7.1 uses the improved version of **reverse** developed in Listing 5.11.

Listing 7.1: Our initial **Phrase** object definition.
palindrome.js

```
// Reverses a string.
function reverse(string) {
  return Array.from(string).reverse().join("");
}

// Returns true for a palindrome, false otherwise.
function palindrome(string) {
  let processedContent = string.toLowerCase();
  return processedContent === reverse(processedContent);
}

// Defines a Phrase object.
function Phrase(content) {
  this.content = content;
}
```

Just as a reality check, it's a good idea to run it in the REPL to catch any syntax errors, etc.:

```
> .load palindrome.js
> phrase = new Phrase("Racecar");
> phrase.content;
'Racecar'
```

As a next step, we'll move the **palindrome** function into the **Phrase** object, adding it as a method. The way to do this is to assign a **function** directly to a **palindrome** property—a method is, in effect, a property that's bound to a function.

Because the desired **content** string is available inside the method as **this.content**, the **palindrome** function no longer needs to take it as an argument. This allows us to change **palindrome** from a function of one variable to a function of zero variables. In other words, we'll change this:

```
function palindrome(string) {
  let processedContent = string.toLowerCase();

  return processedContent === reverse(processedContent);
}
```

to this:

```
this.palindrome = function palindrome() {
  let processedContent = this.content.toLowerCase();

  return processedContent === reverse(processedContent);
}
```

Putting the **palindrome** method into the appropriate place in the **Phrase** method gives the code shown in Listing 7.2. Note that we can use the **reverse** method even inside an object definition; we'll implement an even nicer way of **reverse**-ing strings in Section 7.3.

Listing 7.2: Moving **palindrome** into a method.
palindrome.js

```
// Reverses a string.
function reverse(string) {
  return Array.from(string).reverse().join("");
}
```

```
// Defines a Phrase object.
function Phrase(content) {
  this.content = content;

  // Returns true if the phrase is a palindrome, false otherwise.
  this.palindrome = function palindrome() {
    let processedContent = this.content.toLowerCase();
    return processedContent === reverse(processedContent);
  }
}
```

Loading the file in the REPL shows that it worked (Figure 7.1):[1]

```
> .load palindrome.js
> phrase = new Phrase("Racecar");
> phrase.palindrome();
true
```

The palindrome detector in Listing 7.2 is fairly rudimentary, but we now have a good foundation for building (and testing) a more sophisticated palindrome detector in Chapter 8.

Figure 7.1: A Formula One palindrome.

1. Image courtesy of msyaraafiq/Shutterstock.

7.1.1   Exercise

1. By filling in the code in Listing 7.3, add a **louder** method to the **Phrase** object that returns a LOUDER (all-caps) version of the content. Confirm in the REPL that the result appears as in Listing 7.4.

Listing 7.3: Making the content LOUDER.
`palindrome.js`

```
// Defines a Phrase object.
function Phrase(content) {
  this.content = content;

  // Makes the phrase LOUDER.
  this.louder = function() {
    // FILL IN
  };
}
```

Listing 7.4: Using **louder** in the REPL.

```
> .load palindrome.js
> let p = new Phrase("yo adrian!");
> p.louder();
'YO ADRIAN!'
```

7.2   Prototypes

If you look around for details on JavaScript's object system, you'll quickly find that it is "prototype-based". For example, the Mozilla Developer Network article (https://developer.mozilla.org/en-US/docs/Learn/JavaScript/Objects/Object_prototypes) on object prototypes says the following:

> JavaScript is often described as a **prototype-based language** — each object has a **prototype object**, which acts as a template object that it inherits methods and properties from. An object's prototype object may also have a prototype object, which it inherits methods and properties from, and so on. This is often referred to as a **prototype chain**, and explains why different objects have properties and methods defined on other objects available to them.

This explanation is perfectly correct, but in my experience it can be confusing unless you already know what it's saying, and I don't think anyone ever understood object systems by reading definitions like this one. In my view, generalizing from concrete examples is a better way to go.

Our strategy will be to create a new object called **TranslatedPhrase**, using **Phrase** as its prototype. We'll start by reviewing the **Phrase** object defined in Listing 7.2, which has a **content** property and a **palindrome** method (Listing 7.5).

Listing 7.5: The current state of the **Phrase** object.
palindrome.js

```
// Reverses a string.
function reverse(string) {
  return Array.from(string).reverse().join("");
}

// Defines a Phrase object.
function Phrase(content) {
  this.content = content;

  this.palindrome = function palindrome() {
    let processedContent = this.content.toLowerCase();
    return processedContent === reverse(processedContent);
  }
}
```

Our next step is to factor **processedContent** into its own method, since logically it is a separate operation, and is something we might want to change later on (which indeed will be the case in just a moment). The result appears in Listing 7.6.

Listing 7.6: Moving **processedContent** into a method.
palindrome.js

```
// Reverses a string.
function reverse(string) {
  return Array.from(string).reverse().join("");
}

// Defines a Phrase object.
function Phrase(content) {
  this.content = content;

  // Returns content processed for palindrome testing.
  this.processedContent = function processedContent() {
```

```
    return this.content.toLowerCase();
  }

  // Returns true if the phrase is a palindrome, false otherwise.
  this.palindrome = function palindrome() {
    return this.processedContent() === reverse(this.processedContent());
  }
}
```

Now we're ready to add a second kind of phrase, **TranslatedPhrase**, which has content *and* a translation. We'll start by defining two properties, **content** and **translation**, as seen in Listing 7.7.

Listing 7.7: Defining a **TranslatedPhrase** object.
palindrome.js

```
.
.
.
// Defines a TranslatedPhrase object.
function TranslatedPhrase(content, translation) {
  this.content = content;
  this.translation = translation;
}
```

Now, in order to endow **TranslatedPhrase** with a **palindrome** method, we could copy-and-paste the methods from **Phrase**, like this:

```
function TranslatedPhrase(content, translation) {
  this.content = content;
  this.translation = translation;

  // Returns content processed for palindrome testing.
  this.processedContent = function processedContent() {
    return this.content.toLowerCase();
  }

  // Returns true if the phrase is a palindrome, false otherwise.
  this.palindrome = function palindrome() {
    return this.processedContent() === reverse(this.processedContent());
  }
}
```

But this would result in a terrible duplication of code, a clear violation of the DRY Principle (Box 7.1).

Box 7.1: Don't Repeat Yourself

If you've been poking around the Internet in places where developers talk shop, you might have noticed someone mention staying *DRY*, with "dry" in all caps. They aren't talking about relative moisture levels. What they are talking about is a core principle in programming: *Don't Repeat Yourself*.

The idea behind DRY is that good coding should include as few instances of unnecessary repetition as humanly possible, simply because if you have the same code in a bunch of places, then every time you want to make a change you'll have to update all the different spots in the application where that code is repeated. For example, if you wanted to change the definition of the `palindrome` method, you'd have to make the same change in *every* object that defines it. With only two objects, this might be ugly but manageable, but for a bigger project it would be a nightmare.

Programmers are a special sort of lazy—especially when it comes to doing something repetitive that could be done more efficiently with a little bit of extra programming. To make it easier to be lazy, enterprising programmers spend countless hours creating systems that allow other developers not to have to repeat themselves. We all benefit from developers who at some point decided they were going to work really hard *now* so they could work less hard in the future.

Inheritance is one of these ideas. It allows objects to *inherit* the properties of other objects, so that any methods they have in common need to be defined only once. The result is that we can define a `palindrome` method *once*, and then have other objects inherit `palindrome` from the parent method. In JavaScript, the mechanism for doing this is called the *prototype system*.

Instead, we'll use an important idea in object-oriented programming called *inheritance*, and arrange for **TranslatedPhrase** to inherit the desired **palindrome** method directly from **Phrase**. The way to do this in JavaScript is to set the *prototype* of the second object type equal to an instance of the first; i.e., we need to set **TranslatedPhrase.prototype** to **new Phrase()**, as shown in Listing 7.8.

Listing 7.8: Defining a `TranslatedPhrase` object with a `Phrase` prototype.
palindrome.js

```
.
.
.
// Defines a TranslatedPhrase object.
function TranslatedPhrase(content, translation) {
  this.content = content;
  this.translation = translation;
}
TranslatedPhrase.prototype = new Phrase();
```

Because the **prototype** property of `TranslatedPhrase` has been set to a `Phrase` object, an instance of `TranslatedPhrase` automatically has all the methods of a `Phrase` instance, including **palindrome**. Let's create a variable called **frase** (pronounced "FRAH-seh", Spanish for "phrase") to see how it works (Listing 7.9).

Listing 7.9: Defining a `TranslatedPhrase`.

```
> .load palindrome.js
> let frase = new TranslatedPhrase("recognize", "reconocer");
> frase.palindrome();
false
```

We see that **frase** has a **palindrome()** method as claimed, and that it returns **false** because "recognize" isn't a palindrome.

But what if we wanted to use the *translation* instead of the content for determining whether the translated phrase is a palindrome or not? Because we factored **processedContent** into a separate method (Listing 7.6), we can do this by *overriding* the **processedContent** method in `TranslatedPhrase`, as seen in Listing 7.10.

Listing 7.10: Overriding a method.
palindrome.js

```
// Reverses a string.
function reverse(string) {
  return Array.from(string).reverse().join("");
}
```

```
// Defines a Phrase object.
function Phrase(content) {
  this.content = content;

  // Returns content processed for palindrome testing.
  this.processedContent = function processedContent() {
    return this.content.toLowerCase();
  }

  // Returns true if the phrase is a palindrome, false otherwise.
  this.palindrome = function palindrome() {
    return this.processedContent() === reverse(this.processedContent());
  }
}

// Defines a TranslatedPhrase object.
function TranslatedPhrase(content, translation) {
  this.content = content;
  this.translation = translation;

  // Returns translation processed for palindrome testing.
  this.processedContent = function processedContent() {
    return this.translation.toLowerCase();
  }
}

TranslatedPhrase.prototype = new Phrase();
```

The key point in Listing 7.10 is that we're using **this.translation** instead of **this.content** in the **TranslatedPhrase** version of **processedContent**, so JavaScript knows to use that one instead of the one in **Phrase**. Because the translation "reconocer" *is* a palindrome, we get a different result from the one we got in Listing 7.9, as shown in Listing 7.11. (Note that we need to reassign **frase** in order to use the updated version of **TranslatedPhrase**.)

Listing 7.11: After defining **processedContent** for **TranslatedPhrase**.

```
> .load palindrome.js
> frase = new TranslatedPhrase("recognize", "reconocer");
> frase.palindrome();
true
```

This practice of overriding gives us great flexibility. We can trace the execution of **frase.palindrome()** for the two different cases:

Case 1: Listing 7.8 and Listing 7.9

1. **frase.palindrome()** calls **palindrome()** on the **frase** instance, which is a **TranslatedPhrase**. Since there is no **palindrome()** method in the **TranslatedPhrase** object, JavaScript uses the one from **Phrase**.

2. The **palindrome()** method in **Phrase** calls the **processedContent()** method. Since there is no **processedContent()** method in the **TranslatedPhrase** object, JavaScript uses the one from **Phrase**.

3. The result is to compare the processed version of **this.content** with its own reverse. Since "recognize" isn't a palindrome, the result is **false**.

Case 2: Listing 7.10 and Listing 7.11

1. **frase.palindrome()** calls **palindrome()** on the **frase** instance, which is a **TranslatedPhrase**. As in Case 1, there is no **palindrome()** method in the **TranslatedPhrase** object, so JavaScript uses the one from **Phrase**.

2. The **palindrome()** method in **Phrase** calls the **processedContent()** method. Since there now *is* a **processedContent()** method in the **TranslatedPhrase** object, JavaScript uses the one from **TranslatedPhrase** instead of the one in **Phrase**.

3. The result is to compare the processed version of **this.translation** with its own reverse. Since "reconocer" *is* a palindrome, the result is **true**.

¿Puedes «reconocer» un palíndromo en español? (Can you "reconocer" [recognize] a palindrome in Spanish?) (Figure 7.2).[2]

7.2.1 Exercise

1. After filling in the code in Listing 7.10, both **Phrase** and **TranslatedPhrase** have explicit calls to the **toLowerCase** method. Eliminate this duplication by

---

2. Image courtesy of Archivart/Alamy Stock Photo.

Figure 7.2: Narciso se reconoce. (Narcissus recognizes himself.)

filling in Listing 7.12 to define an appropriate **processor** method that returns the lowercase version of the content.

Listing 7.12: Eliminating duplication with a **processor** method.
palindrome.js

```javascript
// Reverses a string.
function reverse(string) {
  return Array.from(string).reverse().join("");
}

function Phrase(content) {
  this.content = content;

  this.processor = function(string) {
    // FILL IN
  }

  this.processedContent = function processedContent() {
    return this.processor(this.content);
  }
```

```
  // Returns true if the phrase is a palindrome, false otherwise.
  this.palindrome = function palindrome() {
    return this.processedContent() === reverse(this.processedContent());
  }
}

function TranslatedPhrase(content, translation) {
  this.content = content;
  this.translation = translation;

  // Returns translation processed for palindrome testing.
  this.processedContent = function processedContent() {
    return this.processor(this.translation);
  }
}
```

7.3 Modifying Native Objects

As a final step in understanding the JavaScript prototype chain, we're going to learn how to modify native JavaScript objects. Specifically, we're going to add the **reverse** function from Listing 5.11 as a method on **String** objects.

The reader should be warned that what we're about to do is controversial. As the Mozilla Developer Network puts it (https://developer.mozilla.org/en-US/docs /Web/JavaScript/Inheritance_and_the_prototype_chain) (emphasis in original):

> **Bad practice: Extension of native prototypes**
> One misfeature that is often used is to extend **Object.prototype** or one of the other built-in prototypes.
>
> This technique is called monkey patching and breaks *encapsulation*. While used by popular frameworks such as Prototype.js, there is still no good reason for cluttering built-in types with additional *non-standard* functionality.
>
> The **only** good reason for extending a built-in prototype is to backport the features of newer JavaScript engines, like **Array.forEach**.

This advice reminds me of a scene from the movie *Troy*, in which Achilles (Ἀχιλλεύς), the greatest warrior in Greece, is training his close confidant Patroclus (Πάτροκλος, depicted in the film as Achilles' cousin). At one point in their mock swordfight, Achilles switches his wooden training sword from his right hand to his left, holding it up to Patroclus's neck. In response, Patroclus exclaims, "You told me

Figure 7.3: Patroclus and Achilles respectfully decline the advice of the Mozilla Developer Network.

never to change sword hands!" "Yes," replies Achilles. "When you know how to use it, you won't be taking *my* orders."

Likewise, once we know when and why to extend built-in prototypes, we won't be taking orders from the Mozilla Developer Network (Figure 7.3).[3]

The ability to modify native objects is a powerful one, to be sure—a "sharp knife", as it were. But instead of passively accepting MDN's advice, we'll adhere to the philosophy espoused by David Heinemeier Hansson, creator of the Ruby on Rails web framework. As DHH puts it (https://twitter.com/dhh/status/965618592606638080) (Figure 7.4): "Don't let anyone tell you that a powerful technique is too scary or dangerous for you. Let it pique your curiosity instead."

With those caveats in mind, let's see how to add **reverse** to **String**. The trick is to assign a function directly to the **String.prototype** property, as we can see directly in the REPL:

---

3. Image courtesy of Historic Images/Alamy Stock Photo.

Every programmer willing to put in time and care to their craft can learn to wield sharp knives. Those are the programmers I'm interested in helping. Don't let anyone tell you that a powerful technique is too scary or dangerous for you. Let it pique your curiosity instead.

8:06 AM - 19 Feb 2018

Figure 7.4: DHH agrees that sharp knives are OK (when used with care).

```
> String.prototype.reverse = function() {
    return Array.from(this).reverse().join("");
  }
```

With this assignment made, we can now call **reverse** directly on literal strings:

```
> "foobar".reverse();
'raboof'
> "Racecar".reverse();
'racecaR'
```

It also works on string variables:

```
> let string = "Able was I ere I saw Elba";
> string.reverse();
'ablE was I ere I saw elbA'
```

Replacing **reverse** in **palindrome.js** with the code above gives Listing 7.13. (We've removed the **TranslatedPhrase** object now that it's no longer needed for demonstration purposes.)

Listing 7.13: Using the **reverse** method in **processedContent**.

palindrome.js

```
// Adds `reverse` to all strings.
String.prototype.reverse = function() {
  return Array.from(this).reverse().join("");
}

// Defines a Phrase object.
function Phrase(content) {
  this.content = content;

  // Returns content processed for palindrome testing.
  this.processedContent = function processedContent() {
    return this.content.toLowerCase();
  }

  // Returns true if the phrase is a palindrome, false otherwise.
  this.palindrome = function palindrome() {
    return this.processedContent() === this.processedContent().reverse();
  }
}
```

As required, our code still finds palindromes correctly (Figure 7.5):[4]

```
> .load palindrome.js
> let napoleonsLament = new Phrase("Able was I ere I saw Elba");
> napoleonsLament.palindrome();
true
```

As one final comment, it's worth asking whether we might add the **palindrome()** method to **String** itself. The answer depends in part on the culture of the language. Some languages, such as Ruby, are relatively tolerant of adding methods to native objects, as long as the privilege isn't abused. In the case of JavaScript, per MDN's admonition not to add *non-standard* functionality, we'll stick with adding only **reverse**, which arguably belongs in the language as part of the **String** object (and indeed some languages do include a native string **reverse** method). But if you want to add **palindrome()** to **String** yourself, neither I nor Achilles is going to stop you.

---

4. Image courtesy of Everett Collection/Shutterstock.

Figure 7.5: Napoleon Bonaparte was able before being exiled to Elba.

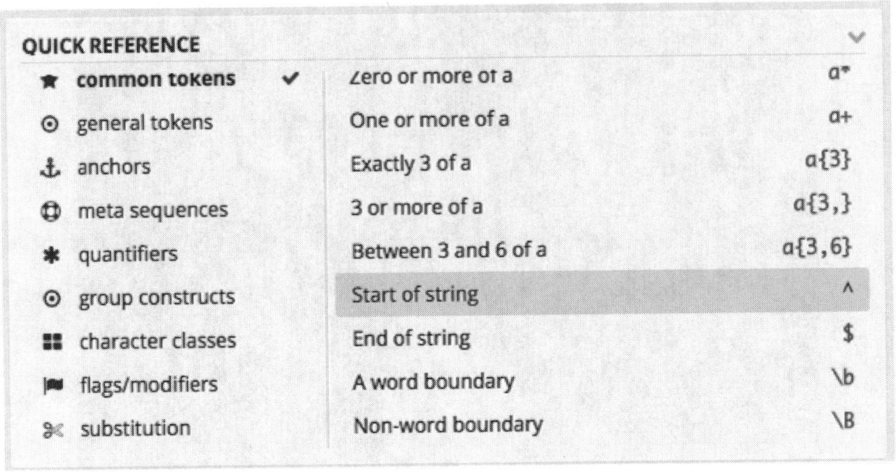

QUICK REFERENCE			⌄
★ **common tokens**	✔	Zero or more of a	*a**
⊙ general tokens		One or more of a	*a*+
⚓ anchors		Exactly 3 of a	*a*{3}
⊕ meta sequences		3 or more of a	*a*{3,}
✳ quantifiers		Between 3 and 6 of a	*a*{3,6}
⊙ group constructs		Start of string	^
▦ character classes		End of string	$
⚑ flags/modifiers		A word boundary	\b
✄ substitution		Non-word boundary	\B

Figure 7.6: Start to end, a blank string is all whitespace.

7.3.1 Exercises

1. Add a **blank** method to the **String** object prototype that returns **true** if the string is empty *or* consists solely of whitespace (spaces, tabs, or newlines). *Hint*: Use a regular expression (Section 4.3.2). You will need the regex syntax for the start and end of a string (Figure 7.6).

2. Using whichever method you prefer (direct indexing or slicing), add a **last** method to the **Array** object prototype that returns the last element of an array. *Hint*: Refer to Section 3.3.

CHAPTER 8

Testing and Test-Driven Development

Although rarely covered in introductory programming tutorials, *automated testing* is one of the most important subjects in modern software development. Accordingly, this chapter includes an introduction to testing in JavaScript, including a first look at *test-driven development*, or TDD.

Test-driven development came up briefly in Section 6.3.3, which promised that we would use testing techniques to add an important capability to finding palindromes, namely, being able to detect complicated palindromes such as "A man, a plan, a canal— Panama!" (Figure 6.7) or "Madam, I'm Adam." (Figure 8.1).[1] This chapter fulfills that promise.

As it turns out, learning how to write JavaScript tests will also give us a chance to learn how to create and use self-contained software packages called *NPM modules*, another valuable modern JavaScript skill.

(In addition to testing NPM modules, testing JavaScript in web applications is certainly possible, but the choices are less standardized, and are often more tightly coupled to the underlying browser and operating system. As a result, this tutorial focuses on the fundamental *ideas* behind testing, thereby serving as preparation for possible browser tests later on.)

Here's our strategy for testing the current palindrome code and extending it to more complicated phrases:

---

1. Image courtesy of Album/Alamy Stock Photo.

Figure 8.1: The Garden of Eden had it all—even palindromes.

1. Set up our system for automated testing (Section 8.1).

2. Write automated tests for the existing **palindrome** functionality (Section 8.2).

3. Write a *failing* test for the enhanced palindrome detector (RED) (Section 8.3).

4. Write (possibly ugly) code to get the test *passing* (GREEN) (Section 8.4).

5. *Refactor* the code to make it prettier, while ensuring that the test suite stays GREEN (Section 8.5).

8.1 Testing Setup

Our testing tool of choice is Mocha (https://mochajs.org/) (Figure 8.2), a powerful testing framework for Node.js. We can install it using the Node Package Manager, or NPM, which comes installed automatically with Node. To install it globally, we use the **npm** command (which is included automatically as part of Node.js) with the **--global** flag:

Figure 8.2: Mocha is a popular and powerful JavaScript testing framework.

```
$ npm install --global mocha
```

(The general rule regarding NPM modules is to install them globally if you just want access to the corresponding executable—in this case, **mocha**—and install them locally (by omitting the **--global** flag) if you want the module to be part of your current project. We'll see an example of the latter case starting in Section 9.1.)

As a second bit of setup, we also have to configure **palindrome.js** as an NPM module itself. This is because (as mentioned briefly in Section 5.3) JavaScript has no native way to include the functionality of one source file into another (an unusual state of affairs for a programming language, which in this case is due to JavaScript's roots in the browser). In this case, we want to be able to use our palindrome detector in web pages (Chapter 9) and in shell scripts (Chapter 10). Luckily, Node includes a special function called **require** to accomplish this task, so that the code

```
require(<module name>)
```

will include the functionality of the corresponding module in the current application.

Our palindrome detector will exist as a standalone module; that is, it will be self-contained and suitable for inclusion into other programs (web pages, shell scripts, or even other modules). As a result, we'll place all the code for the module in a separate directory, called **palindrome**:

```
$ cd ~/repos/
$ mkdir palindrome
$ cd palindrome
```

Next, we'll get a head start on our **palindrome** module by copying the **pal-indrome.js** file developed in previous sections to the file **index.js**, which is the standard name for the main file in an NPM module:

```
$ cp ~/repos/js_tutorial/palindrome.js index.js
```

We'll adapt this file into the full palindrome detector throughout the rest of this chapter.

Since the directory is now nonempty, we can put it under version control with Git:

```
$ git init
$ git add -A
$ git commit -m "Initialize repository"
```

At this point, I recommend creating a public repository for the module at GitHub by following the instructions in Section 1.2.1. This will also give you a GitHub repo URL for use in the next step.

To get us started with a new module, the **npm** program comes with a helpful command called **npm init**, which includes a series of interactive questions. I suggest running **npm init** and filling in the values by referring to Listing 8.1; especially make sure to use **mocha** as the "test command" and 0.1.0 for the version number (Box 8.1). (We'll learn more about the versioning process when we publish our module in Section 8.5.) Also note that I've scoped the package name using my standard username (**mhartl**), yielding

```
"name": "mhartl-palindrome"
```

instead of

```
"name": "palindrome"
```

This is done so that everyone reading this tutorial can create a separate module, so you should substitute a unique username in place of **mhartl** in Listing 8.1.

Listing 8.1: Initializing an NPM module.

```
$ npm init
package name: (mhartl-palindrome)
version: (0.1.0)
description: Palindrome detector
entry point: (index.js)
test command: mocha
git repository: https://github.com/mhartl/mhartl-palindrome
keywords: palindrome learn-enough javascript
author: Michael Hartl
license: (ISC)
About to write to /Users/mhartl/repos/palindrome/package.json:

{
  "name": "mhartl-palindrome",
  "version": "0.1.0",
  "description": "Palindrome detector",
  "main": "index.js",
  "scripts": {
    "test": "mocha"
  },
  "repository": {
    "type": "git",
    "url": "https://github.com/mhartl/mhartl-palindrome"
  },
  "author": "Michael Hartl",
  "license": "ISC"
}
```

The result of Listing 8.1 is a file called **package.json** that records the configuration for our module using JavaScript Object Notation, or JSON (usually pronounced "JAY-sun" or "JAY-sahn").

Box 8.1: Semver

You might have noticed in Listing 8.1 that we've used the version number 0.1.0 for our new module. The leading zero indicates that our package is at an early stage, often called "beta" (or even "alpha" for very early-stage projects).

We can indicate updates by incrementing the middle number in the version, e.g., from 0.1.0 to 0.2.0, 0.3.0, etc. Bugfixes are represented by incrementing the rightmost number, as in 0.2.1, 0.2.2, and a mature version (suitable for use by others, and which may not be backward-compatible with prior versions) is indicated by version 1.0.0.

After reaching version 1.0.0, further changes follow this same general pattern: 1.0.1 would represent minor changes (a "patch release"), 1.1.0 would represent new (but backward-compatible) features (a "minor release"), and 2.0.0 would represent major or backward-incompatible changes (a "major release").

These numbering conventions are known as *semantic versioning*, or *semver* for short. For more information, see the NPM article on how to use semantic versioning (https://docs.npmjs.com/about-semantic-versioning).

The final step in preparing our module for testing is to *export* the **Phrase** object so that it can be used in other files. (We'll see how to *import* **Phrase** in Section 8.2.) All that's required is a single **export** line, which we can place at the top of the file (Listing 8.2).

Listing 8.2: Exporting a module.
~/repos/palindrome/index.js

```js
module.exports = Phrase;

// Adds `reverse` to all strings.
String.prototype.reverse = function() {
  return Array.from(this).reverse().join("");
}

// Defines a Phrase object.
function Phrase(content) {
  this.content = content;

  // Returns content processed for palindrome testing.
  this.processedContent = function processedContent() {
    return this.content.toLowerCase();
  }

  // Returns true if the phrase is a palindrome, false otherwise.
  this.palindrome = function palindrome() {
    return this.processedContent() === this.processedContent().reverse();
  }
}
```

8.1.1 Exercise

1. As indicated (https://docs.npmjs.com/about-package-readme-files) in the NPM
   guide "How to Publish & Update a Package" (https://docs.npmjs.com/packages-
   and-modules/contributing-packages-to-the-registry), it's a good practice to
   include a "README" file with information about the module. Create a file
   with the required name **readme.md** and fill it with information about the module.
   You can use my readme (https://github.com/mhartl/mhartl-palindrome#phrase-
   object-with-palindrome-detector) as a reference if you like.

8.2 Initial Test Coverage

With the preparation from Section 8.1 done, we're now ready to get started with our
automated tests. We'll start by making a **test** directory and **test.js** file:

```
$ mkdir test/
$ touch test/test.js
```

Now we need to fill **test.js** with the test code for the **palindrome**
method. We begin by including two NPM modules in **test.js** using the **require**
function, which is how Node imports functionality from an external file. The first is
an *assertion library* that lets us assert that things are true in our tests, and the second is
the **Phrase** object itself:

```
let assert = require("assert");
let Phrase = require("../index.js");
```

Next, we'll use two functions from **assert**, called **describe** and **it**. The
describe function takes a string and another function. For example, to describe the
Phrase object, we can start like this:

```
describe("Phrase", function() {
```

Next, since we're going to test **palindrome** inside the **Phrase** object, we'll *nest* a
second call to **describe**. In particular, as we saw briefly in Section 3.2, the usual
way to indicate an object method is to use a hash mark # in front of the method
(**Phrase#palindrome**), which we can indicate in the test as follows:

```
describe("Phrase", function() {
  describe("#palindrome", function() {
```

Finally, inside the **describe** functions we'll add a call to the **it** function, which also takes a string and a function:

```
describe("Phrase", function() {

  describe("#palindrome", function() {

    it("should return false for a non-palindrome", function() {
      let nonPalindrome = new Phrase("apple");
      assert(!nonPalindrome.palindrome());
    });
    .
    .
    .
```

Here we've used **assert** to assert that **"apple"** should *not* be a palindrome (Figure 8.3),[2] where "not" is indicated with an exclamation point ("bang") **!** as usual (Section 2.4.1).

In similar fashion, we can test a plain palindrome (one that's literally the same forward and backward) with another call to **it**:

```
it("should return true for a plain palindrome", function() {
  let plainPalindrome = new Phrase("racecar");
  assert(plainPalindrome.palindrome());
});
```

Combining the code from the above discussion gives us our initial test file, as shown in Listing 8.3.

Listing 8.3: Our initial test suite.
~/repos/palindrome/test/test.js

```
let assert = require("assert");
let Phrase = require("../index.js");

describe("Phrase", function() {
```

---

2. Image courtesy of Glayan/Shutterstock.

Figure 8.3: The word "apple": not a palindrome.

```
describe("#palindrome", function() {

  it("should return false for a non-palindrome", function() {
    let nonPalindrome = new Phrase("apple");
    assert(!nonPalindrome.palindrome());
  });

  it("should return true for a plain palindrome", function() {
    let plainPalindrome = new Phrase("racecar");
    assert(plainPalindrome.palindrome());
  });
  });
});
```

Now for the real test (so to speak). To run our set of tests, or *test suite*, we simply run **npm test** (Listing 8.4), which (because of the configuration in Section 8.1) uses the **mocha** command under the hood.

Listing 8.4: The test suite after the initial setup. GREEN

```
$ npm test

  Phrase
    #palindrome()
      ✓ should return false for a non-palindrome
      ✓ should return true for a plain palindrome

  2 passing (6ms)
```

The tests should be GREEN, indicating that they are now in a passing state.

8.2.1 Pending Tests

Before moving on, we'll add a couple of *pending* tests, which are placeholders/ reminders for tests we want to write. The way to write a pending test is simply to use **it** with only a string argument (omitting the **function**), as shown in Listing 8.5.

Listing 8.5: Adding two pending tests.
~/repos/palindrome/test/test.js

```
let assert = require("assert");
let Phrase = require("../index.js");

describe("Phrase", function() {

  describe("#palindrome", function() {

    it("should return false for a non-palindrome", function() {
      let nonPalindrome = new Phrase("apple");
      assert(!nonPalindrome.palindrome());
    });

    it("should return true for a plain palindrome", function() {
      let plainPalindrome = new Phrase("racecar");
      assert(plainPalindrome.palindrome());
    });
    it("should return true for a mixed-case palindrome");

    it("should return true for a palindrome with punctuation");
  });
});
```

We can see the result of Listing 8.5 by rerunning the test suite (Listing 8.6).

Listing 8.6: The pending tests from Listing 8.5. GREEN

```
$ npm test

  Phrase
    #palindrome
      ✓ should return false for a non-palindrome
      ✓ should return true for a plain palindrome
      - should return true for a mixed-case palindrome
      - should return true for a palindrome with punctuation

  2 passing (6ms)
  2 pending
```

Now Mocha displays indications that there are two pending tests. (Sometimes people speak of a test suite with pending tests as being YELLOW, in analogy with the red-yellow-green color scheme of traffic lights.)

Filling in the test for a mixed-case palindrome is left as an exercise (with a solution shown in the next section), while filling in the second pending test is the subject of Section 8.3 and Section 8.4.

8.2.2 Exercises

1. By filling in the code in Listing 8.7, add a test for a mixed-case palindrome like "RaceCar". Is the test suite still GREEN?

2. In order to make 100% sure that the tests are testing what we *think* they're testing, it's a good practice to get to a failing state (RED) by intentionally *breaking* the tests. Change the application code to break each of the existing tests in turn, and then confirm that they are GREEN again once the original code has been restored. An example of code that breaks the test in the previous exercise (but not the other tests) appears in Listing 8.8. (One advantage of writing the tests *first* is that this RED–GREEN cycle happens automatically.)

Listing 8.7: Adding a test for a mixed-case palindrome.

~/repos/palindrome/test/test.js

```
        .
        .
        .
    it("should return true for a mixed-case palindrome", function() {
      let mixedCase = new Phrase("RaceCar");
      // Fill in this line
    });
        .
        .
        .
```

Listing 8.8: Intentionally breaking a test. RED

~/repos/palindrome/index.js

```
module.exports = Phrase;

// Adds `reverse` to all strings.
String.prototype.reverse = function() {
  return Array.from(this).reverse().join("");
}

// Defines a Phrase object.
function Phrase(content) {
  this.content = content;

  // Returns content processed for palindrome testing.
  this.processedContent = function processedContent() {
    return this.content;
  }

  // Returns true if the phrase is a palindrome, false otherwise.
  this.palindrome = function palindrome() {
    return this.processedContent() === this.processedContent().reverse();
  }
}
```

8.3 Red

In this section, we'll take the important first step toward being able to detect more complex palindromes like "Madam, I'm Adam." and "A man, a plan, a canal—Panama!". Unlike the previous strings we've encountered, these phrases—which contain both spaces and punctuation—aren't strictly palindromes in a literal sense, even if we ignore capitalization. Instead of testing the strings as they are, we have to figure out a way to select only the letters, and then see if the resulting letters are the same forward and backward.

The code to do this is fairly tricky, but the tests for it are simple. This is one of the situations where test-driven development particularly shines (Box 8.2). We can write our simple tests, thereby getting to RED, and then write the application code any way we want to get to GREEN (Section 8.4). At that point, with the tests protecting us against undiscovered errors, we can change the application code with confidence (Section 8.5).

Box 8.2: When to Test

When deciding when and how to test, it's helpful to understand *why* to test. In my view, writing automated tests has three main benefits:

1. Tests protect against *regressions*, where a functioning feature stops working for some reason.
2. Tests allow code to be *refactored* (i.e., changing its form without changing its function) with greater confidence.
3. Tests act as a *client* for the application code, thereby helping determine its design and its interface with other parts of the system.

Although none of the above benefits *require* that tests be written first, there are many circumstances where test-driven development (TDD) is a valuable tool to have in your kit. Deciding when and how to test depends in part on how comfortable you are writing tests; many developers find that, as they get better at writing tests, they are more inclined to write them first. It also depends on how difficult the test is relative to the application code, how precisely the desired features are known, and how likely the feature is to break in the future.

In this context, it's helpful to have a set of guidelines on when we should test first (or test at all). Here are some suggestions based on my own experience:

- When a test is especially short or simple compared to the application code it tests, lean toward writing the test first.
- When the desired behavior isn't yet crystal clear, lean toward writing the application code first, then write a test to codify the result.

- Whenever a bug is found, write a test to reproduce it and protect against regressions, then write the application code to fix it.
- Write tests before refactoring code, focusing on testing error-prone code that's especially likely to break.

We'll start by writing a test for a palindrome with punctuation, which just parallels the tests from Listing 8.3:

```
it("should return true for a palindrome with punctuation", function() {
  let punctuatedPalindrome = new Phrase("Madam, I'm Adam.");
  assert(punctuatedPalindrome.palindrome());
});
```

The updated test suite appears in Listing 8.9, which also includes the solution to the exercise in Listing 8.7 (Figure 8.4[3]). (For brevity, only the new **let**s and assertions are highlighted in Listing 8.9, but you should include the **it**s as well.)

Figure 8.4: "RaceCar" is still a palindrome (ignoring case).

---

3. Image courtesy of msyaraafiq/Shutterstock.

Listing 8.9: Adding a test for a punctuated palindrome. RED

~/repos/palindrome/test/test.js

```
let assert = require("assert");
let Phrase = require("../index.js");

describe("Phrase", function() {

  describe("#palindrome", function() {

    it("should return false for a non-palindrome", function() {
      let nonPalindrome = new Phrase("apple");
      assert(!nonPalindrome.palindrome());
    });

    it("should return true for a plain palindrome", function() {
      let plainPalindrome = new Phrase("racecar");
      assert(plainPalindrome.palindrome());
    });

    it("should return true for a mixed-case palindrome", function() {
      let mixedCase = new Phrase("RaceCar");
      assert(mixedCase.palindrome());
    });

    it("should return true for a palindrome with punctuation", function() {
      let punctuatedPalindrome = new Phrase("Madam, I'm Adam.");
      assert(punctuatedPalindrome.palindrome());
    });
  });
});
```

As required, the test suite is now RED, as seen in Listing 8.10.

Listing 8.10: The test suite after adding the test in Listing 8.9. RED

```
$ npm test

  Phrase
    #palindrome
      ✓ should return false for a non-palindrome
      ✓ should return true for a plain palindrome
      ✓ should return true for a mixed-case palindrome
      1) should return true for a palindrome with punctuation


  3 passing (8ms)
```

```
1 failing

1) Phrase
     #palindrome
        should return true for a palindrome with punctuation:

   AssertionError [ERR_ASSERTION]: false == true
   + expected - actual

   -false
   +true
```

At this point, we can start thinking about how to write the application code and get to GREEN. Our strategy will be to write a **letters** method for the **Phrase** object that returns only the letters in the content string. In other words, the code

```
new Phrase("Madam, I'm Adam.").letters();
```

should evaluate to this:

```
MadamImAdam
```

(Note here that we can actually call **letters()** on a **new Phrase**—JavaScript knows to create the new object instance before calling the **letters()** method on it.) Getting to this state will allow us to use our current palindrome detector to determine whether the original phrase is a palindrome or not.

Having made this specification, we can now write a simple test for **letters**. We could follow the pattern from previous tests and assert (strict) equality directly (Listing 8.11).

Listing 8.11: Asserting strict equality directly.

```
let punctuatedPalindrome = new Phrase("Madam, I'm Adam.");
assert(punctuatedPalindrome.letters() === "MadamImAdam");
```

It turns out, though, that the **assert** module has native support for this kind of comparison (as seen in the official documentation (https://www.npmjs.com /package/assert)), leading to assertions of the form shown in Listing 8.12.

Listing 8.12: Using a native assertion.

```
assert.strictEqual(<actual>, <expected>);
```

As we'll see in a moment, it's generally preferable to use native assertions when possible, since doing so leads to more helpful messages for failed tests. For the sake of such failing test messages, it's also important to include the arguments in the "actual, expected" order shown above.

In the present case, the "actual" result is **punctuatedPalindrome.letters()**, and the "expected" value is **"MadamImAdam"**, so we can fill in the assertion as follows:

```
let punctuatedPalindrome = new Phrase("Madam, I'm Adam.");
assert.strictEqual(punctuatedPalindrome.letters(), "MadamImAdam");
```

Adding a new **describe** function for **letters** (and adding the hash symbol # to indicate that we're testing **Phrase#letters**) leads to the code shown in Listing 8.13.

Listing 8.13: Adding a test for the **letters** method. RED
~/repos/palindrome/test/test.js

```
describe("Phrase", function() {
  .
  .
  .
  describe("#palindrome", function() {
    .
    .
    .
  });

  describe("#letters", function() {
    it("should return only letters", function() {
      let punctuatedPalindrome = new Phrase("Madam, I'm Adam.");
      assert.strictEqual(punctuatedPalindrome.letters(), "MadamImAdam");
    });
  });
});
```

Because the **letters** method doesn't exist at all, the current failing message isn't all that helpful, as seen in Listing 8.14.

Listing 8.14: The initial failing message for `letters`. RED

```
$ npm test
  .
  .
  .
  2) Phrase
       #letters
         should return only letters:
     TypeError: punctuatedPalindrome.letters is not a function
```

We can get to a more useful RED state by adding a *stub* for `letters`: a method that doesn't work, but at least exists. For simplicity, we'll simply return the content of the phrase, as shown in Listing 8.15.

Listing 8.15: A stub for the `letters` method. RED
~/repos/palindrome/index.js

```
module.exports = Phrase;
  .
  .
  .
function Phrase(content) {
  .
  .
  .
  // Returns the letters in the content.
  this.letters = function letters() {
    return this.content;    // stub return value
  }

  // Returns true if the phrase is a palindrome, false otherwise.
  this.palindrome = function palindrome() {
    return this.processedContent() === this.processedContent().reverse();
  }
}
```

As promised, the error message is now quite helpful, as seen in Listing 8.16.

Listing 8.16: A more helpful error message. RED

```
$ npm test
```

```
Phrase
  #palindrome
    ✓ should return false for a non-palindrome
    ✓ should return true for a plain palindrome
    ✓ should return true for a mixed-case palindrome
    1) should return true for a palindrome with punctuation
  #letters
    2) should return only letters


3 passing (9ms)
2 failing

1) Phrase
     #palindrome
       should return true for a palindrome with punctuation:

     AssertionError [ERR_ASSERTION]: false == true
     + expected - actual

     -false
     +true

     at Context.<anonymous> (test/test.js:25:7)

2) Phrase
     #letters
       should return only letters:

     AssertionError [ERR_ASSERTION]: 'Madam, Iḿ Adam.' === 'MadamImAdam'
     + expected - actual

     -Madam, I'm Adam.
     +MadamImAdam
```

With our two RED tests capturing the desired behavior, we're now ready to move on to the application code and try getting it to GREEN.

8.3.1 Exercises

1. What is the error message when using the direct **===** assertion shown in Listing 8.11? Why is this less useful than the message in Listing 8.16?

2. What happens if you reverse the actual and expected values (Listing 8.12) in Listing 8.16? Why is the resulting error message confusing?

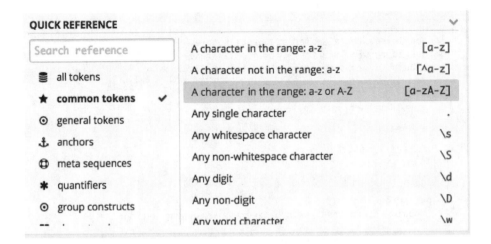

Figure 8.5: The exact regex we need.

8.4 Green

Now that we have RED tests to capture the enhanced behavior of our palindrome detector, it's time to make them GREEN. Part of the philosophy of TDD is to get them passing without worrying too much at first about the quality of the implementation. Once the test suite is GREEN, we can polish it up without introducing regressions (Box 8.2).

The main challenge is implementing **letters**, which returns a string of the letters (but not any other characters) making up the **content** of a **Phrase**. In other words, we need to select the characters that match a certain pattern. This sounds like a job for regular expressions (Section 4.3).

At times like these, using an online regex matcher with a regex reference like the one shown in Figure 4.5 is an excellent idea. Indeed, sometimes they make things a little *too* easy, such as when the reference has the exact regex you need (Figure 8.5).

Let's test it in the console to make sure it satisfies our criteria:

```
$ node
> !!"M".match(/[a-zA-Z]/);
true
> !!"d".match(/[a-zA-Z]/);
true
> !!",".match(/[a-zA-Z]/);
false
```

Lookin' good!

We're now in a position to build up an array of characters that matches upper- or lowercase letters. The most straightforward way to do this is with a **for** loop and the **charAt** method we first saw in Section 2.6. We'll start with an array for the letters, and then iterate through the content string, **push**ing each character onto the array (Section 3.4.2) if it matches the letter regex:

```
let theLetters = [];
for (let i = 0; i < this.content.length; i++) {
  if (this.content.charAt(i).match(/[a-zA-Z]/)) {
    theLetters.push(this.content.charAt(i));
  }
}
```

At this point, **theLetters** is an array of letters, which can be **join**ed on the empty string to form a string of the letters in the original string:

```
return theLetters.join("");
```

Putting everything together gives the **Phrase#letter** method in Listing 8.17 (with a highlight added to indicate the beginning of the new method).

Listing 8.17: A working **letters** method (but full suite still RED).
~/repos/palindrome/index.js

```
module.exports = Phrase;

// Adds `reverse` to all strings.
String.prototype.reverse = function() {
  return Array.from(this).reverse().join("");
}

// Defines a Phrase object.
function Phrase(content) {
  this.content = content;

  // Returns content processed for palindrome testing.
  this.processedContent = function processedContent() {
    return this.content.toLowerCase();
  }

  // Returns the letters in the content.
```

```
// For example:
//   new Phrase("Hello, world!").letters() === "Helloworld"
this.letters = function letters() {
  let theLetters = [];
  for (let i = 0; i < this.content.length; i++) {
    if (this.content.charAt(i).match(/[a-zA-Z]/)) {
      theLetters.push(this.content.charAt(i));
    }
  }
  return theLetters.join("");
}

// Returns true if the phrase is a palindrome, false otherwise.
this.palindrome = function palindrome() {
  return this.processedContent() === this.processedContent().reverse();
}
}
```

Although the full test suite is still RED, our **letters** test should now be GREEN, as seen in the highlighted line in Listing 8.18.

Listing 8.18: A RED suite but a GREEN **letters** test.

```
$ npm test

  Phrase
    #palindrome
      ✓ should return false for a non-palindrome
      ✓ should return true for a plain palindrome
      ✓ should return true for a mixed-case palindrome
      1) should return true for a palindrome with punctuation
    #letters
      ✓ should return only letters

  4 passing (8ms)
  1 failing

  1) Phrase
       #palindrome
         should return true for a palindrome with punctuation:

      AssertionError [ERR_ASSERTION]: false == true
      + expected - actual

      -false
      +true
```

We can get the final RED test to pass by replacing **content** with **letters()** in the **processedContent** method. The result appears in Listing 8.19.

Listing 8.19: A working **palindrome** method. GREEN

~/repos/palindrome/index.js

```
module.exports = Phrase;

// Adds `reverse` to all strings.
String.prototype.reverse = function() {
  return Array.from(this).reverse().join("");
}

// Defines a Phrase object.
function Phrase(content) {
  this.content = content;

  // Returns content processed for palindrome testing.
  this.processedContent = function processedContent() {

    return this.letters().toLowerCase();
  }

  // Returns the letters in the content.
  // For example:
  //   new Phrase("Hello, world!").letters() === "Helloworld"
  this.letters = function letters() {
    let theLetters = [];
    for (let i = 0; i < this.content.length; i++) {
      if (this.content.charAt(i).match(/[a-zA-Z]/)) {
        theLetters.push(this.content.charAt(i));
      }
    }
    return theLetters.join("");
  }

  // Returns true if the phrase is a palindrome, false otherwise.
  this.palindrome = function palindrome() {
    return this.processedContent() === this.processedContent().reverse();
  }
}
```

Figure 8.6: Our detector finally understands Adam's palindromic nature.

The result of Listing 8.19 is a GREEN test suite (Figure 8.6), as seen in Listing 8.20.

Listing 8.20: The test suite after Listing 8.19. GREEN

```
$ npm test

  Phrase
    #palindrome
      ✓ should return false for a non-palindrome
      ✓ should return true for a plain palindrome
      ✓ should return true for a mixed-case palindrome
      ✓ should return true for a palindrome with punctuation
    #letters
      ✓ should return only letters


  5 passing (6ms)
```

It may not be the prettiest code in the world, but this GREEN test suite means our code is working!

8.4.1 Exercise

1. By **require**-ing the **palindrome** module in a Node REPL, verify by hand that the **Phrase#palindrome** code can successfully detect palindromes of the form "Madam, I'm Adam." (You may have to quit and restart the REPL to refresh all relevant object definitions.) *Hint*: Use the same **require** command as in the second line of Listing 8.3 but with **./** in place of **../**.

8.5 Refactor

Although the code in Listing 8.19 is now working, as evidenced by our GREEN test suite, it relies on a rather cumbersome (if straightforward) **for** loop, and there's some duplication as well. In this section, we'll *refactor* our code, which is the process of changing the form of code without changing its function.

By running our test suite after any significant changes, we'll catch any regressions quickly, thereby giving us confidence that the final form of the refactored code is still correct. Throughout this section, I suggest making changes incrementally and running the test suite after each change to confirm that the suite is still GREEN.

We start by observing that there's some duplication in Listing 8.19: The expression

```
this.content.charAt(i)
```

appears twice. This suggests eliminating the duplication by binding it to a variable using **let**:

```
this.letters = function letters() {
  let theLetters = [];
  for (let i = 0; i < this.content.length; i++) {

    let character = this.content.charAt(i);
    if (character.match(/[a-zA-Z]/)) {
      theLetters.push(character);

    }
  }
  return theLetters.join("");
}
```

As another bit of polish, we can simplify the regex by using **i** after **/.../** to make a case-insensitive match, while also binding it to a named constant to make its purpose clearer:

```
const letterRegex = /[a-z]/i;

for (let i = 0; i < this.content.length; i++) {
  let character = this.content.charAt(i);

  if (character.match(letterRegex)) {

    theLetters.push(character);
  }
}
```

Per Section 5.4, it's usually better to use a **forEach** loop when we can. We can do this using the techniques from Listing 5.15, as follows:

```
const letterRegex = /[a-z]/i;

Array.from(this.content).forEach(function(character) {

  if (character.match(letterRegex)) {
    theLetters.push(character);
  }
});
```

Note that we were able to remove the **let** for the **character** variable since now it comes for free as part of the **forEach** loop's function parameter.

We've got one final refactoring to do, but for reference the full state of the application code appears in Listing 8.21.

Listing 8.21: A refactored **letters** method. GREEN
~/repos/palindrome/index.js

```
module.exports = Phrase;

// Adds `reverse` to all strings.
String.prototype.reverse = function() {
  return Array.from(this).reverse().join("");
}

// Defines a Phrase object.
function Phrase(content) {
  this.content = content;

  // Returns content processed for palindrome testing.
  this.processedContent = function processedContent() {
    return this.letters().toLowerCase();
  }
```

```
// Returns the letters in the content.
// For example:
//   new Phrase("Hello, world!").letters() === "Helloworld"
this.letters = function letters() {
  let theLetters = [];
  const letterRegex = /[a-z]/i;
  Array.from(this.content).forEach(function(character) {
    if (character.match(letterRegex)) {
      theLetters.push(character);
    }
  });
  return theLetters.join("");
}

// Returns true if the phrase is a palindrome, false otherwise.
this.palindrome = function palindrome() {
  return this.processedContent() === this.processedContent().reverse();
}
}
```

The result of running the test suite is gratifying, as seen in Listing 8.22.

Listing 8.22: The test suite after refactoring with **forEach**. GREEN

```
$ npm test

Phrase
  #palindrome
    ✓ should return false for a non-palindrome
    ✓ should return true for a plain palindrome
    ✓ should return true for a mixed-case palindrome
    ✓ should return true for a palindrome with punctuation
  #letters
    ✓ should return only letters


5 passing (6ms)
```

It's still GREEN! The changes above involved lots of tricky and error-prone manipulations, so a GREEN test suite gives us confidence that we didn't introduce any
regressions.

   To motivate one final refactoring, we can note that the form of the code in Listing 8.21 is similar to that in Listing 6.4 from Section 6.2: We initialize an empty array
and then **push** to it in a **forEach** loop. In Listing 6.5, we used functional programming

via the **filter** method to convert that loop to a single line, and we can do exactly the same thing here.

As a quick refresher, let's drop into the REPL:

```
> Array.from("Madam, I'm Adam.");
[ 'M', 'a', 'd', 'a', 'm', ',', ' ', 'I', '\'', 'm', ' ',
'A', 'd', 'a', 'm', '.' ]
> Array.from("Madam, I'm Adam").filter(c => c.match(/[a-z]/i));
[ 'M', 'a', 'd', 'a', 'm', 'I', 'm', 'A', 'd', 'a', 'm' ]
> Array.from("Madam, I'm Adam").filter(c => c.match(/[a-z]/i)).join("");
'MadamImAdam'
```

We see here how combining method chaining (Section 5.3) with functional programming makes it easy to filter and join the letter characters in a string.

Applying **filter** to the code in Listing 8.21, we can condense the **letters** method into a single line, as shown in Listing 8.23. (It could arguably be improved by retaining the **lettersRegEx** constant from Listing 8.21, but I find the austerity of a one-line function to be nearly impossible to resist.)

Listing 8.23: Refactoring **letters** down to a single line. GREEN
~/repos/palindrome/index.js

```
module.exports = Phrase;

// Adds `reverse` to all strings.
String.prototype.reverse = function() {
  return Array.from(this).reverse().join("");
}

// Defines a Phrase object.
function Phrase(content) {
  this.content = content;

  // Returns content processed for palindrome testing.
  this.processedContent = function processedContent() {
    return this.letters().toLowerCase();
  }

  // Returns the letters in the content.
  // For example:
  //   new Phrase("Hello, world!").letters() === "Helloworld"
  this.letters = function letters() {
    return Array.from(this.content).filter(c => c.match(/[a-z]/i)).join("");
  }
}
```

```
  // Returns true if the phrase is a palindrome, false otherwise.
  this.palindrome = function palindrome() {
    return this.processedContent() === this.processedContent().reverse();
  }
}
```

As noted in Chapter 6, functional programs are harder to build up incrementally, which is one reason why it's so nice to have a test suite to check that it had its intended effect (Listing 8.24).[4]

Listing 8.24: The test suite after a functional refactoring. GREEN

```
$ npm test

  Phrase
    #palindrome
      ✓ should return false for a non-palindrome
      ✓ should return true for a plain palindrome
      ✓ should return true for a mixed-case palindrome
      ✓ should return true for a palindrome with punctuation
    #letters
      ✓ should return only letters


  5 passing (6ms)
```

Huzzah! Our test suite still passes, so our one-line **letters** method works.

This is a major improvement, but in fact there's one more refactoring that represents a great example of the power of JavaScript. Recall from Section 4.3 that **match** can use a regex to return an array from a string. By combining with the global flag **g** from Section 4.5, we can select the letters directly:

```
> "Madam, I'm Adam.".match(/[a-z]/gi);
[ 'M', 'a', 'd', 'a', 'm', 'I', 'm', 'A', 'd', 'a', 'm' ]
> "Madam, I'm Adam.".match(/[a-z]/gi).join("");
'MadamImAdam'
```

---

4. IRL, I would probably write the **Phrase#letters** method by first writing the tests we saw in Section 8.3, and then try for a functional solution right away. If I failed at that, I would backtrack, do it an easier (loopier) way, and then make another run at a functional solution after getting the test suite GREEN. (I find this sort of backtracking to be especially necessary with the **reduce** method we met in Section 6.3.)

By matching on the same regex we've been using throughout this section and then joining on the empty string, we've nearly replicated the functionality of the **letters** method! There's only one subtlety, which is that when there are *no* letters, the result is **null**:

```
> "1234".match(/[a-z]/gi);
null
> "1234".match(/[a-z]/gi).join("");
TypeError: Cannot read property 'join' of null
```

We can fix this with the **||** ("or") operator (Section 2.4), which uses a method known as "short-circuit evaluation".

If the first element in a list of **||** statements evaluates as **true**, the evaluation "short-circuits" and JavaScript immediately returns that element. If the first element is **false**, JavaScript evaluates the next one, and so on until it finds one that is **true**, and then returns the final element (or the final element if all of the elements are **false**). This means that we can handle the case above like this:

```
> null || []
[]
```

Here JavaScript sees **null**, evaluates it as **false**, and then moves on to **[]**, which is **true** and so gets returned.

We can combine this idea with **match** as follows:

```
> ("1234".match(/[a-z]/gi) || []);
[]
> ("1234".match(/[a-z]/gi) || []).join("");
''
```

Using this technique, we can simplify the application code even further, as shown in Listing 8.25.

Listing 8.25: Replacing **letters** with a **match**.
~/repos/palindrome/index.js

```
module.exports = Phrase;

// Adds `reverse` to all strings.
String.prototype.reverse = function() {
  return Array.from(this).reverse().join("");
```

```
}

// Defines a Phrase object.
function Phrase(content) {
  this.content = content;

  // Returns content processed for palindrome testing.
  this.processedContent = function processedContent() {
    return this.letters().toLowerCase();
  }

  // Returns the letters in the content.
  // For example:
  //    new Phrase("Hello, world!").letters() === "Helloworld"
  this.letters = function letters() {
    return (this.content.match(/[a-z]/gi) || []).join("");
  }

  // Returns true if the phrase is a palindrome, false otherwise.
  this.palindrome = function palindrome() {
    return this.processedContent() === this.processedContent().reverse();
  }
}
```

Note that we don't have a test for the important case where **match** returns **null**; adding this is left as an exercise (Section 8.5.2).

One more run of the test suite confirms that everything is still copacetic (Figure 8.7), as seen in Listing 8.26.

Listing 8.26: The test suite after a final refactoring. GREEN

```
$ npm test

  Phrase
    #palindrome
      ✓ should return false for a non-palindrome
      ✓ should return true for a plain palindrome
      ✓ should return true for a mixed-case palindrome
      ✓ should return true for a palindrome with punctuation
    #letters
      ✓ should return only letters


  5 passing (6ms)
```

Figure 8.7: Still a palindrome after all our work.

8.5.1 Publishing the NPM Module

Having finished a refactored version of our **palindrome** module, we're now ready for the final step, which is to publish the module publicly so that it can be included into other projects (such as the site in Chapter 9). Luckily, NPM makes this amazingly easy.

First, we should make a Git commit and push up the remote repository:

```
$ git add -A
$ git commit -m "Finish working and refactored palindrome method"
$ git push
```

To publish the NPM module, you'll need to add yourself as a user (unless you're already a member), which is simple using **npm adduser** (where you should use your own name, username, and email address):

```
$ npm adduser Michael Hartl
Username: mhartl
Password:
Email: (this IS public) michael@michaelhartl.com
Logged in as mhartl on https://registry.npmjs.org/
```

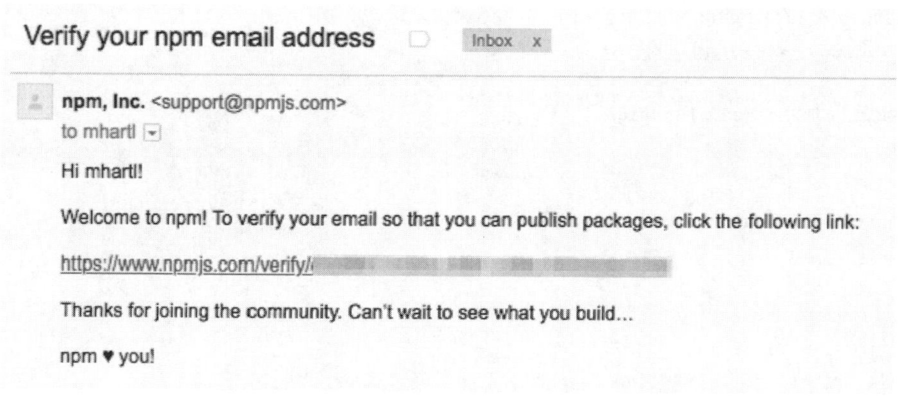

Figure 8.8: Verifying your NPM email.

NPM requires that you verify your email address before allowing you to publish (presumably to make it more difficult to abuse their system), so you should check email and click on the verification link before proceeding (Figure 8.8).

With that, we're ready to go! Just use **npm publish** to publish the module to the public NPM list:

```
$ npm publish
```

For any future revisions, you can simply increment the version number in **package.json** according to the rules of semver (Section 8.1).

8.5.2   Exercises

1. Eliminate the **|| []** part of Listing 8.25 and confirm that the tests are still GREEN. This is a problem, because in fact the application code is now broken. Add the test shown in Listing 8.27 to catch the error and confirm that it's RED, then restore **|| []** to get the suite back to GREEN.

2. Reintroduce the **lettersRegEx** variable from Listing 8.21 (now with the added **g** flag from Listing 8.25) and apply it to the functional version of the **letters** method by filling in the code shown in Listing 8.28. Does the test suite still pass?

Listing 8.27: Testing a string with no letters. RED

~/repos/palindrome/test/test.js

```
describe("Phrase", function() {
  .
  .
  .
  describe("#palindrome", function() {
    .
    .
    .
  });

  describe("#letters", function() {
    it("should return only letters", function() {
      let punctuatedPalindrome = new Phrase("Madam, I'm Adam.");
      assert.strictEqual(punctuatedPalindrome.letters(), "MadamImAdam");
    });

    it("should return the empty string on no match", function() {
      let noLetters = new Phrase("1234.56");
      assert.strictEqual(noLetters.letters(), "");
    });
  });
});
```

Listing 8.28: Reintroducing the **lettersRegEx** variable. GREEN

~/repos/palindrome/index.js

```
this.letters = function letters() {
  const lettersRegEx = /[a-z]/gi;
  return // FILL IN
}
```

CHAPTER 9

Events and DOM Manipulation

In this chapter, we return to JavaScript's native environment and put our newly created Node module to work in the browser. Specifically, we'll be making a simple single-page JavaScript application that takes in a string from the user and indicates whether or not that string is a palindrome.

Our approach involves gradually increasing levels of sophistication, starting with a simple "hello, world"–style proof-of-concept (Section 9.1). We'll then add a prompt/-alert design that will motivate the introduction of *event listeners* (Section 9.2). In Section 9.3, we'll replace the alert with dynamic HTML inserted on the page itself—our first example of manipulating the Document Object Model tree. Finally, in Section 9.4 we'll add an HTML *form*, which is a more convenient method for entering data than a JavaScript prompt.

9.1 A Working Palindrome Page

To get started with our palindrome detector, we'll create both an HTML file and our site's main JavaScript file, called **palindrome.html** and **main.js**, respectively:

```
$ cd ~/repos/js_tutorial
$ touch palindrome.html main.js
```

As in Chapter 1, we'll make a minimal "hello, world" app just to prove that everything is basically working. To do this, we need to install the **\<username\>-palindrome** module created in Section 8.1:

```
$ npm install <username>-palindrome      # Replace <username> with your username.
```

If for any reason you didn't complete Section 8.1, you can use my version of the module, **mhartl-palindrome**.

To use the **Phrase** object exported by the module (Listing 8.2), all we need to do is edit **main.js** and use **let** to bind the name **Phrase** to the result of the **require** function, as shown in Listing 9.1.

Listing 9.1: Adding a proof-of-concept.
main.js

```
let Phrase = require("<username>-palindrome");

alert(new Phrase("Madam, I'm Adam.").palindrome());
```

Listing 9.1 also includes an **alert**, which if it works will tell us that the **require** succeeded.

Recall from Section 5.2 that we can include external JavaScript files using the **src** attribute of the **script** tag (Listing 5.5):

```
<script src="filename.js"></script>
```

You might think that we could just include **main.js** directly, like this:

```
<script src="main.js"></script>
```

Unfortunately, because browsers don't support **require**, this won't work. Instead, we need to use an NPM module called **browserify** (Google "require node module into browser"):

```
$ npm install --global browserify
```

The **browserify** utility takes our offline code and bundles it up in a way that browsers can understand, as shown in Listing 9.2.

Listing 9.2: Using `browserify` to prepare a JavaScript bundle for the browser.

```
$ browserify main.js -o bundle.js
```

Using the **-o** (output file) flag, Listing 9.2 arranges to create a file called **bundle.js** that *can* be included in a browser.[1] (How does browserify do this? I have no idea. Being able to use modules whose inner workings are mysterious is an important part of technical sophistication.)

Note: Making changes in **main.js** but forgetting to rerun **browserify** is a common source of errors, so be sure to try rerunning Listing 9.2 if you ever find that your expected changes aren't showing up on the page. I also suggest looking at the watchify (https://www.npmjs.com/package/watchify) package, which is designed to re-build the bundled version automatically.

At this point, our JavaScript is properly bundled for use on a web page, so we can include it using the **src** attribute as developed in Section 5.2. The resulting **palindrome.html**, which includes a minimal HTML skeleton as well, appears in Listing 9.3.

Listing 9.3: Creating the palindrome page, including the JavaScript source.
palindrome.html

```html
<!DOCTYPE html>
<html>
  <head>
    <title>Palindrome Tester</title>
    <meta charset="utf-8">
    <script src="bundle.js"></script>
  </head>
  <body>
    <h1>Palindrome Tester</h1>
  </body>
</html>
```

The result should be a working alert, as shown in Figure 9.1. If things don't work on your system, follow the suggestions in Box 5.1 to resolve the discrepancy.

---

1. The **browserify** program defaults to dumping the results to the screen (STDOUT), so redirecting (https://www.learnenough.com/command-line-tutorial/manipulating_files#sec-redirecting_and_appending) via **browserify main.js > bundle.js** works as well.

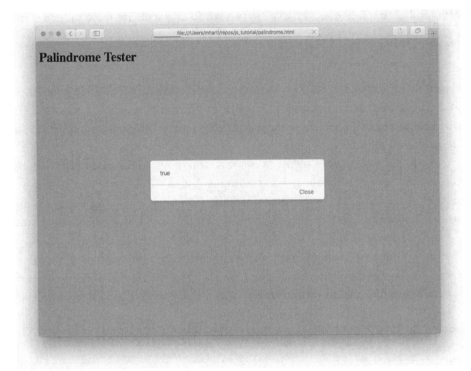

Figure 9.1: Confirming that the module has been loaded.

Amazingly, we can already get a working (if rudimentary) palindrome detector working. All we need to do is use the **prompt** function, which prompts the user for some input (and returns the result):

```
let Phrase = require("<username>-palindrome");
let string = prompt("Please enter a string for palindrome testing:");
```

The user's input is automatically returned, allowing us to create a new **Phrase** instance and test whether it's a palindrome or not:

```
let phrase = new Phrase(string);

if (phrase.palindrome()) {
  alert(`"${phrase.content}" is a palindrome!`);
} else {
  alert(`"${phrase.content}" is not a palindrome.`)
}
```

Putting everything together gives the result shown in Listing 9.4.

Listing 9.4: Our first working palindrome detector.
main.js

```
let Phrase = require("<username>-palindrome");

let string = prompt("Please enter a string for palindrome testing:");
let phrase = new Phrase(string);

if (phrase.palindrome()) {
  alert(`"${phrase.content}" is a palindrome!`);
} else {
  alert(`"${phrase.content}" is not a palindrome.`)
}
```

All we need to do now is rerun **browserify** and reload the browser:

```
$ browserify main.js -o bundle.js
```

Refreshing **palindrome.html** now immediately prompts us for a string, as shown in Figure 9.2.

The user experience may not be all that great, but, as seen in Figure 9.3, it actually works!

9.1.1 Exercise

1. By following the steps from Section 1.2.1, deploy the palindrome detector to production. It might be necessary to add a file to tell GitHub Pages to treat the site as ordinary HTML instead of using the Jekyll static site builder (which sometimes causes errors when processing Node modules), as shown in Listing 9.5. (Some readers have reported that it currently works without this step.) Does the code work on the live site?

Listing 9.5: Telling GitHub Pages not to use the Jekyll static site builder.

```
$ touch .nojekyll
$ git add -A
$ git commit -m "Prevent Jekyll build"
```

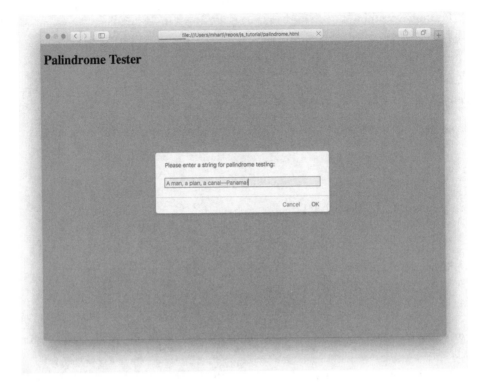

Figure 9.2: A string prompt.

9.2 Event Listeners

In Section 9.1, we somewhat miraculously got a live palindrome detector working, but the user experience wasn't all that great: Users visiting the page are immediately hit with a prompt, without even a chance to see what the page is about.

In this section, we'll make the palindrome page a little friendlier by adding a *button* that gives the user the option to initiate the action. It's also nicer for detecting palindromes more than once, since users will be able to click the button again rather than having to refresh the entire page.

Our first step is to add the button itself, as shown in Listing 9.6, which shows how to use the HTML **button** tag.

Figure 9.3: Alerted to a valid palindrome.

Listing 9.6: Adding a button.
palindrome.html

```
<!DOCTYPE html>
<html>
  <head>
    <title>Palindrome Tester</title>
    <meta charset="utf-8">
    <script src="bundle.js"></script>
  </head>
  <body>
    <h1>Palindrome Tester</h1>
    <button id="palindromeTester">Is it a palindrome?</button>
  </body>
</html>
```

Note that the button in Listing 9.6 uses a CSS id. This is in line with the recommendations discussed (https://www.learnenough.com/css-and-layout-tutorial /style-of-style#sec-css_why) in *Learn Enough CSS & Layout to Be Dangerous* (https://www.learnenough.com/css-and-layout), which recommended not using ids for styling (preferring classes instead), and reserving them for use in things like JavaScript applications (a time that now has come!).

After refreshing the page, we see the button appear (Figure 9.4).

As you can confirm by clicking it, the button currently does nothing, but we can change that using a JavaScript *event listener*, which is a piece of code that waits for a particular event to happen and then responds appropriately. In this case, the response will be the palindrome test itself, so we'll factor the corresponding code from Listing 9.4 into a separate function, as shown in Listing 9.7.

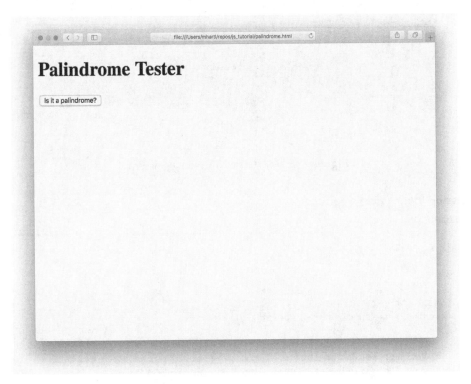

Figure 9.4: A wild button appears.

Listing 9.7: Factoring the palindrome tester into a function.
main.js

```
function palindromeTester() {
  let string = prompt("Please enter a string for palindrome testing:");
  let phrase = new Phrase(string);

  if (phrase.palindrome()) {
    alert(`"${phrase.content}" is a palindrome!`);
  } else {
    alert(`"${phrase.content}" is not a palindrome.`)
  }
}
```

Next, we'll create a special object that represents the button itself. The way to do this is to use the powerful **querySelector** function, which lets us find an element in the page's DOM using its id:[2]

```
let button = document.querySelector("#palindromeTester");
```

Note here that JavaScript knows to look for a CSS id (and not a CSS class) because **#palindromeTester** starts with a hash symbol #. Recall (https://www.learnenough .com/css-and-layout-tutorial/style-of-style#sec-naming_things) from *Learn Enough CSS & Layout to Be Dangerous* that is the same notation to select a CSS id in CSS itself.

(The **querySelector** method is a rare case where Googling can lead you astray; as of this writing, searching for javascript find element by id leads mainly to **getElementById**, which does in fact work, but which is not as powerful and flexible as the newer **querySelector** method.)

Having created an object to represent the button, we can now add the event listener and set it to listen for a "click" using **addEventListener**:

```
let button = document.querySelector("#palindromeTester");
button.addEventListener("click", function() {
  palindromeTester();
});
```

---

2. I originally intended to cover the popular jQuery library in this tutorial, but using it does introduce some overhead and a third-party dependency, so I was pleased to discover that **querySelector** and the closely related **querySelectorAll** (Section 11.2) have made vanilla JavaScript plenty powerful for our purposes.

The first argument here is the kind of event, while the second is a function that will be executed when the click happens. (A function of this sort that executes when something else happens is called a *callback*.) In this case, we could actually have written

```
let button = document.querySelector("#palindromeTester");
button.addEventListener("click", palindromeTester);
```

but we've used an anonymous function instead to emphasize the general case where there might be more than one line.

Putting everything together, the resulting **main.js** appears as in Listing 9.8.

Listing 9.8: The initial event listener code.

main.js

```
let Phrase = require("<username>-palindrome");

function palindromeTester() {
  let string = prompt("Please enter a string for palindrome testing:");
  let phrase = new Phrase(string);

  if (phrase.palindrome()) {
    alert(`"${phrase.content}" is a palindrome!`);
  } else {
    alert(`"${phrase.content}" is not a palindrome.`)
  }
}

let button = document.querySelector("#palindromeTester");
button.addEventListener("click", function() {
  palindromeTester();
});
```

Running Listing 9.2, refreshing the page, and clicking the button shows that… still nothing happens. Taking a look at the console gives us a hint why (Figure 9.5). Somehow, the **button** object isn't being defined.

The solution to this mystery also addresses something we glossed over when building up to Listing 9.8: Namely, what is **document**? The answer is that **document** (surprise!) represents the document itself. The problem we're facing is that, at the time that **main.js** (via **bundle.js**) gets loaded, *the document content hasn't finished*

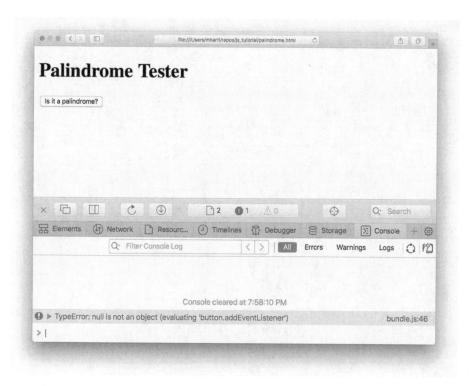

Figure 9.5: An unexpected `null` object.

loading yet. As a result, while the **document** object exists, there is not yet an element with id **palindromeTester**, so the **querySelector** in Listing 9.8 turns up a big fat **null**. When we try calling **addEventListener** on this **null**, it raises the error shown in Figure 9.5.

This is a common issue when programming in JavaScript, and the solution is to use a *second* listener, one that waits for the Document Object Model content to be loaded.

As noted briefly in Chapter 1, the Document Object Model, or DOM, is the hierarchical model used to describe the contents of a web page (Figure 9.6). When rendering a page, the browser constructs the DOM using the content of the page, and fires off an event notification when the DOM content is loaded. For our button listener to work, this event—called, appropriately enough, **"DOMContentLoaded"**— needs a listener of its own:

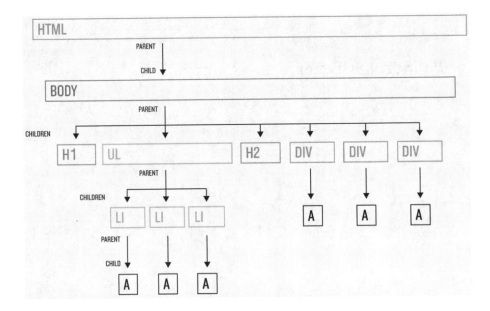

Figure 9.6: The DOM.

```
document.addEventListener("DOMContentLoaded", function() {
  let button = document.querySelector("#palindromeTester");
  button.addEventListener("click", function() {
    palindromeTester();

  });
});
```

Let's put this expanded code into **main.js** (Listing 9.9) and see what happens.

Listing 9.9: An event listener for the loading of the DOM.

main.js

```
let Phrase = require("<username>-palindrome");

function palindromeTester() {
  let string = prompt("Please enter a string for palindrome testing:");
  let phrase = new Phrase(string);

  if (phrase.palindrome()) {
```

```
    alert(`"${phrase.content}" is a palindrome!`);
  } else {
    alert(`"${phrase.content}" is not a palindrome.`)
  }
}
document.addEventListener("DOMContentLoaded", function() {
  let button = document.querySelector("#palindromeTester");
  button.addEventListener("click", function() {
    palindromeTester();
  });
});
```

Rerunning Listing 9.2, refreshing the browser, and clicking the button shows that it's working! The result appears in Figure 9.7.

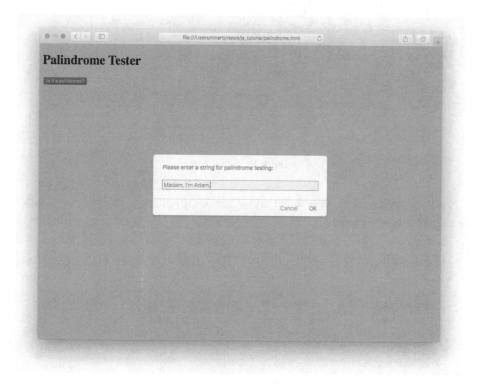

Figure 9.7: Clicking the button after waiting for the DOM to load.

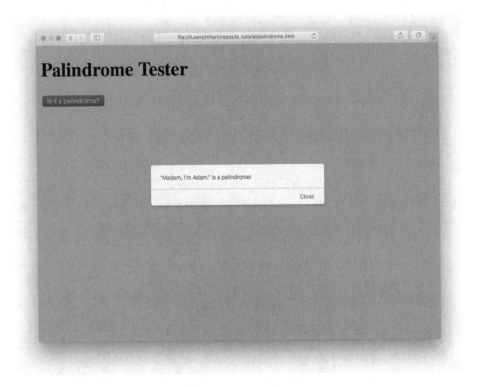

Figure 9.8: Still an alert.

As with the initial version in Section 9.1, the current page displays the results in an **alert**, as seen in Figure 9.8.

This is an excellent start. In Section 9.3, we'll learn how to display the result in the HTML itself.

9.2.1 Exercise

1. The most common way to handle a button is to put it in an HTML *form* (discussed further in Section 9.4). Confirm using the code in Listing 9.10 and Listing 9.11 that it's possible to combine a form, a button, and a listener on the **submit** event to achieve the same behavior as a plain button. (Don't forget to rerun **browserify** to update **bundle.js**.)

Listing 9.10: Adding a simple HTML form.

palindrome.html

```html
<!DOCTYPE html>
<html>
  <head>
    <title>Palindrome Tester</title>
    <meta charset="utf-8">
    <script src="bundle.js"></script>
  </head>
  <body>
    <h1>Palindrome Tester</h1>
    <form id="palindromeTester">
      <button type="submit">Is it a palindrome?</button>
    </form>
  </body>
</html>
```

Listing 9.11: Listening for the **submit** event.

main.js

```javascript
let Phrase = require("<username>-palindrome");

function palindromeTester() {
  let string = prompt("Please enter a string for palindrome testing:");
  let phrase = new Phrase(string);

  if (phrase.palindrome()) {
    alert(`"${phrase.content}" is a palindrome!`);
  } else {
    alert(`"${phrase.content}" is not a palindrome.`)
  }
}

document.addEventListener("DOMContentLoaded", function() {
  let form = document.querySelector("#palindromeTester");
  form.addEventListener("submit", function() {
    palindromeTester();
  });
});
```

9.3 Dynamic HTML

We left off in Section 9.2 with a working palindrome detector, but displaying the results in an **alert** is a little cumbersome. In this section, we'll improve the design by updating the page HTML directly. (Accepting input via a **prompt** is also cumbersome; we'll address that issue in Section 9.4.)

To prepare for this, let's add another heading and a paragraph with a CSS id for the result (Listing 9.12).

Listing 9.12: Adding HTML for a palindrome result.
palindrome.html

```
<!DOCTYPE html>
<html>
  <head>
    <title>Palindrome Tester</title>
    <meta charset="utf-8">
    <script src="bundle.js"></script>
  </head>
  <body>
    <h1>Palindrome Tester</h1>

    <button id="palindromeTester">Test palindrome</button>
    <h2>Result</h2>

    <p id="palindromeResult"></p>
  </body>
</html>
```

Note that the paragraph in Listing 9.12 is *empty*; this is because we're going to fill its contents dynamically with JavaScript.

Amazingly, updating our code to use dynamic HTML instead of an alert requires adding only one line, while making minor edits to two others. We first need to use the same **querySelector** method from Listing 9.9 to grab the HTML element with the **palindromeResult** id:

```
function palindromeTester() {
  let string = prompt("Please enter a string for palindrome testing:");
  let phrase = new Phrase(string);

  let palindromeResult = document.querySelector("#palindromeResult");
```

```
  if (phrase.palindrome()) {
    alert(`"${phrase.content}" is a palindrome!`);
  } else {
    alert(`"${phrase.content}" is not a palindrome.`)
  }
}
```

Then, instead of using an **alert**, we can simply assign the notification strings to the **innerHTML** attribute of the **palindromeResult** object:

```
function palindromeTester() {
  let string = prompt("Please enter a string for palindrome testing:");
  let phrase = new Phrase(string);
  let palindromeResult = document.querySelector("#palindromeResult");

  if (phrase.palindrome()) {

    palindromeResult.innerHTML = `"${phrase.content}" is a palindrome!`;

  } else {

    palindromeResult.innerHTML = `"${phrase.content}" is not a palindrome.`;

  }
}
```

The full **main.js** now appears as in Listing 9.13.

Listing 9.13: Adding the notification to the result area.
main.js

```
let Phrase = require("<username>-palindrome");

function palindromeTester() {
  let string = prompt("Please enter a string for palindrome testing:");
  let phrase = new Phrase(string);
  let palindromeResult = document.querySelector("#palindromeResult");

  if (phrase.palindrome()) {
    palindromeResult.innerHTML = `"${phrase.content}" is a palindrome!`;
  } else {
    palindromeResult.innerHTML = `"${phrase.content}" is not a palindrome.`;
  }
}

document.addEventListener("DOMContentLoaded", function() {
  let button = document.querySelector("#palindromeTester");
```

```
  button.addEventListener("click", function() {
    palindromeTester();
  });
});
```

Upon rerunning Listing 9.2 and refreshing the browser, the result area is now
ready to display the notification previously seen in the alert (Figure 9.9).

Let's see if our detector can correctly identify one of the most ancient palindromes,
the so-called Sator Square first found in the ruins of Pompeii (Figure 9.10).[3] (Author-
ities differ on the exact meaning of the Latin words in the square, but the likeliest
translation is "The sower [farmer] Arepo holds the wheels with effort.")

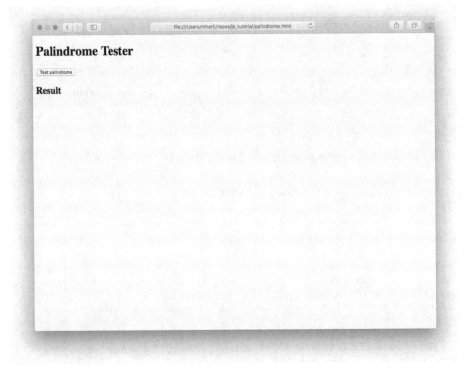

Figure 9.9: The result area.

---

3. Image courtesy of CPA Media Pte Ltd/Alamy Stock Photo.

Figure 9.10: A Latin palindrome from the lost city of Pompeii.

Clicking the button and entering "SATOR AREPO TENET OPERA ROTAS" (Figure 9.11) leads to the results being displayed directly in the HTML, as seen in Figure 9.12.

9.3.1 Exercise

1. In order to make the result in Figure 9.12 easier to read, make the palindrome itself bold using the **strong** tag, as in " '**SATOR AREPO TENET OPERA ROTAS**' is a palindrome!"

9.4 Form Handling

As a final touch, in this section we'll replace the **prompt** used in previous sections with a more natural *HTML form*. Although form handling in general requires having a back-end web application on the server (such as that provided by Sinatra (https://www.learnenough.com/ruby) or Rails (https://www.railstutorial.org/)), we can fake it with JavaScript by adding an event listener to intercept the resulting **"submit"** event.

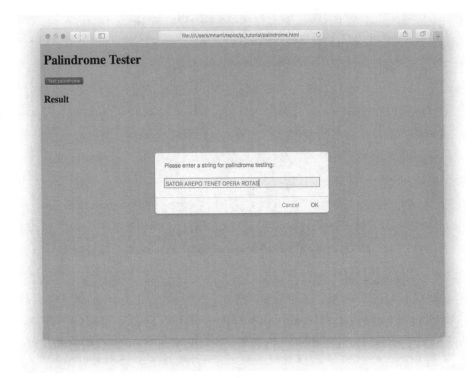

Figure 9.11: A Latin palindrome.

The first step is to wrap the **button** tag (Listing 9.12) in a form:

```
<form id="palindromeTester">
  <textarea name="phrase" rows="10" cols="30"></textarea>
  <br>
  <button type="submit">Is it a palindrome?</button>
</form>
```

Here we've transferred the CSS id to the **form** tag itself, and have introduced the HTML **textarea** tag (10 rows tall and 30 columns wide), while also identifying the **button** as being of type **"submit"**. Note also that the **textarea** has a **name** attribute (with value **"phrase"**); this will become important in a moment.

Placing the form on our palindrome page leads to the code shown in Listing 9.14. The result appears in Figure 9.13.

Figure 9.12: HTML dynamicus.

Listing 9.14: Adding a form to the palindrome page.
palindrome.html

```
<!DOCTYPE html>
<html>
  <head>
    <title>Palindrome Tester</title>
    <meta charset="utf-8">
    <script src="bundle.js"></script>
  </head>
  <body>
    <h1>Palindrome Tester</h1>
    <form id="palindromeTester">
      <textarea name="phrase" rows="10" cols="30"></textarea>
      <br>
      <button type="submit">Is it a palindrome?</button>
    </form>
```

```
  <h2>Result</h2>

  <p id="palindromeResult"></p>

  </body>
</html>
```

Since we've changed the event type, we need to update our listener, changing from **"click"** to **"submit"**:

```
document.addEventListener("DOMContentLoaded", function() {

  let tester = document.querySelector("#palindromeTester");
  tester.addEventListener("submit", function(event) {
    palindromeTester(event);
  });
});
```

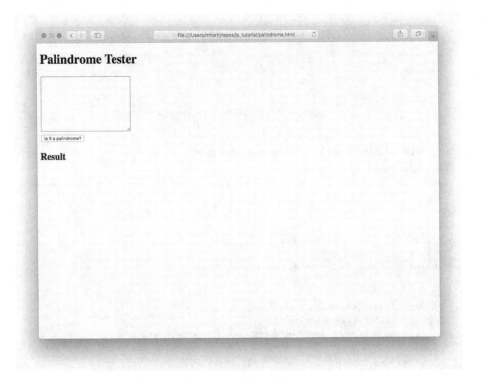

Figure 9.13: Our palindrome page with a fancy new form.

Note that we've also added the **event** parameter to the function argument and when calling **palindromeTester**; more on this in a moment.

Then, in the **palindromeTester** method, we have to make two minor changes. The first involves preventing the *default behavior* of the form, which is to submit information back to the server. Since our "server" is just a static web page, we can't handle such a submission, so we need to prevent this default behavior as follows:

```
function palindromeTester(event) {
  event.preventDefault();
  .
  .
  .
}
```

Here **event** is a special object that JavaScript provides for just this sort of case.

The second change is that, instead of grabbing the phrase string from a **prompt**, we'll get it directly from the form submission. This is where the **name** attribute from the **textarea** in Listing 9.14 comes in: We can access the phrase from the *target* of the **event**. In this case, the **event** target is just a **form** object, so **event.target** is the form itself. Moreover, because of the **name="phrase"** key–value pair in the **textarea** of the form, **event.target** has an attribute whose *value* is the submitted string. In other words, if we entered, say, the phrase "Madam, I'm Adam.", we could extract the value as follows:

```
event.target.phrase.value    // would be "Madam, I'm Adam."
```

Applying this to the **palindromeTester** function and combining with the new listener gives the result shown in Listing 9.15. By the way, the inclusion of **event** in **function(event)** isn't necessary on some systems, but should be included for maximum cross-browser compatibility.

Listing 9.15: Handling form submission in JavaScript.
main.js

```
let Phrase = require("<username>-palindrome");
function palindromeTester(event) {
  event.preventDefault();

  let phrase = new Phrase(event.target.phrase.value);
```

```
let palindromeResult = document.querySelector("#palindromeResult");

if (phrase.palindrome()) {
  palindromeResult.innerHTML = `"${phrase.content}" is a palindrome!`;
} else {
  palindromeResult.innerHTML = `"${phrase.content}" is not a palindrome.`;
}
}

document.addEventListener("DOMContentLoaded", function() {
  let tester = document.querySelector("#palindromeTester");
  tester.addEventListener("submit", function(event) {
    palindromeTester(event);
  });
});
```

Rerunning Listing 9.2, refreshing, and filling the textarea with one of my favorite looooong palindromes (Figure 9.14) gives the result shown in Figure 9.15.[4]

And with that—"A man, a plan, a canoe, pasta, heros, rajahs, a coloratura, maps, snipe, percale, macaroni, a gag, a banana bag, a tan, a tag, a banana bag again (or a camel), a crepe, pins, Spam, a rut, a Rolo, cash, a jar, sore hats, a peon, a canal—Panama!"—we're done with the web version of our JavaScript palindrome detector. Whew!

9.4.1 Exercises

1. Confirm by submitting an empty form that an empty string is currently considered to be a palindrome (Figure 9.16). This is true in a vacuous sense, but it's probably not the behavior we want.

2. To fix this issue, follow the procedure outlined in Box 8.2 and write a RED test asserting that the empty string is *not* a palindrome (Listing 9.16), then confirm that the application code in Listing 9.17 gets the test GREEN.

3. Bump the version number using the guidelines in Box 8.1, publish your new module as in Section 8.5.1, and then update it using the **npm update** command (Listing 9.18). Does your application now correctly identify **""** as not being a palindrome (Figure 9.17)? (*Hint*: Don't forget to rerun Listing 9.2.)

---

4. The amazingly long palindrome in Figure 9.14 was created in 1983 by pioneering computer scientist Guy Steele with the aid of a custom program.

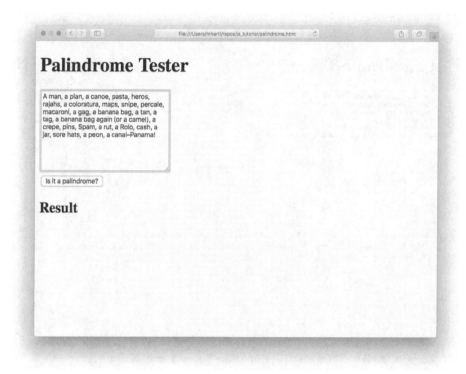

Figure 9.14: Entering a long string in the form's textarea field.

Listing 9.16: Template for asserting that the empty string isn't a palindrome. RED
~/repos/palindrome/test/test.js

```
let assert = require("assert");
let Phrase = require("../index.js");

describe("Phrase", function() {

  describe("#palindrome", function() {
    .
    .
    .
    it("should return false for an empty string", function() {
      let emptyPhrase = new Phrase("");
      assert(FILL_IN);
    });
  }
}
```

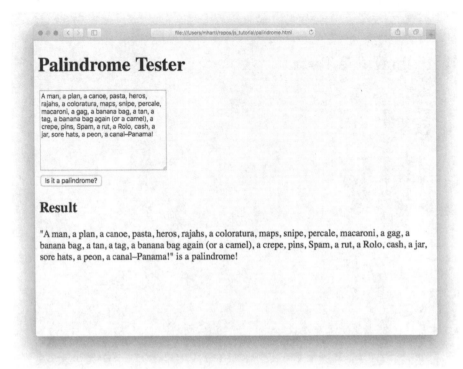

Figure 9.15: That long string is a palindrome!

Listing 9.17: Application code for Listing 9.16. GREEN

~/repos/palindrome/index.js

```
module.exports = Phrase;

// Adds `reverse` to all strings.
String.prototype.reverse = function() {
  return Array.from(this).reverse().join("");
}

function Phrase(content) {
  this.content = content;
  .
  .
  .
  // Returns true if the phrase is a palindrome, false otherwise.
  this.palindrome = function palindrome() {
    if (this.processedContent()) {
      return this.processedContent() === this.processedContent().reverse();
```

```
    } else {
      return false;
    }
  }
}
```

Listing 9.18: Updating an NPM module.

```
$ npm update <username>-palindrome
```

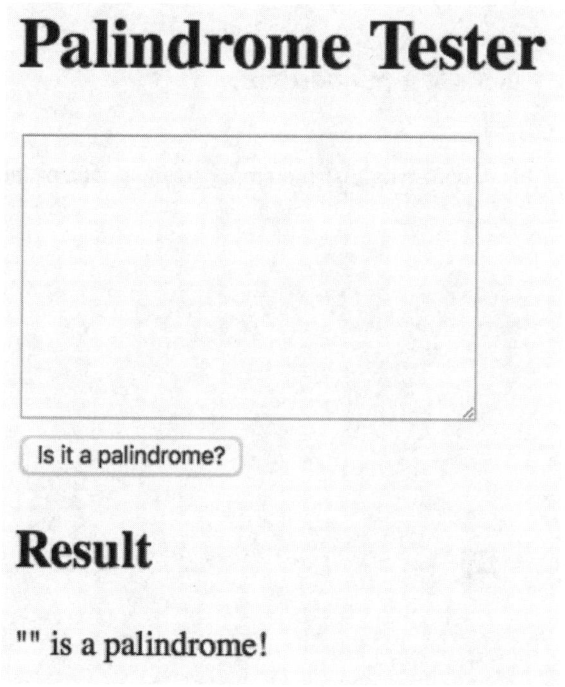

Palindrome Tester

Is it a palindrome?

Result

"" is a palindrome!

Figure 9.16: Oops—our application thinks the empty string is a palindrome!

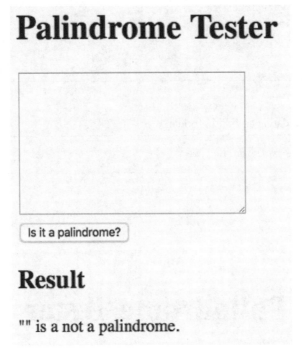

Figure 9.17: Confirming that the empty string is *not* a palindrome.

CHAPTER 10
Shell Scripts with Node.js

In this chapter, we'll return to the world of the command line and use Node.js to write three *shell scripts* of increasing sophistication. This use of JavaScript is currently less common than JavaScript in the browser, but it can be expected to grow as JavaScript (especially via Node and NPM) continues to expand past its original web-programming niche. These programs also serve as a useful foundation for similar programs written in languages more traditionally thought of as "scripting languages", such as Perl, Python, and Ruby.

Perhaps surprisingly, we'll discover en route that the DOM manipulation skills developed in Chapter 9 are still useful in shell scripts. Indeed, we'll extend our capabilities significantly, in exactly the direction needed for the more advanced manipulations used in Chapter 11.

The first program (Section 10.1) shows how to use JavaScript to read and process the contents of a file from the filesystem. The program in Section 10.2 then shows how to accomplish the similar feat of reading the contents of a URL. (This has personal meaning to me, as I distinctly remember the first time I wrote an automated program to read and process text from the Web, which at the time seemed truly miraculous.) Finally, in Section 10.3, we'll write a real-life utility program adapted from one I once wrote for myself; it includes an introduction (alluded to above) to DOM manipulation in a context outside of a web browser.

10.1 Reading from Files

Our first task is to read and process the contents of a file. The example is simple by design, but it demonstrates the necessary principles, and gives you the background needed to read more advanced documentation.

We'll start by using **curl** to download a file of simple phrases (note that this should be in the **js_tutorial** directory we used prior to Chapter 8, not the palindrome package directory):

```
$ cd ~/repos/js_tutorial/
$ curl -OL https://cdn.learnenough.com/phrases.txt
```

As you can confirm by running **less phrases.txt** at the command line, this file contains a large number of phrases—some of which (surprise!) happen to be palindromes.

Our specific task is to write a palindrome detector that iterates through each line in this file and prints out any phrases that are palindromes (while ignoring others). To do this, we'll need to open the file and read its contents.

When I started writing this tutorial, *I* didn't know how to do this in Java-Script. But I applied my technical sophistication (Box 1.1) and dropped "node open file" into Google. (Why not "javascript open file"? That might have worked, but I suspected—correctly, as it turned out—that JavaScript's browser-centric origins made "node" a more promising search term.) This search quickly turned up the File System module **fs**, which solves exactly the problem we have:

```
$ npm install --global fs
```

The documentation for File System can be a bit overwhelming, so I dug a little deeper and found the post "Reading a file with Node.js" (https://code-maven.com/reading-a-file-with-nodejs), which described the exact solution to our problem. Adapted to our current filename and programming conventions (e.g., **let** in place of **var**, double quotes), it looks like this in the REPL:

```
> let fs = require("fs");
> let text = fs.readFileSync("phrases.txt", "utf-8");
```

Here we've opted for the "Sync" (synchronous) version of the **readFile** function, mainly because we have no need to run more than one of these programs at a time (which is what "asynchronous" is for). We've also included (following the blog post) a second argument to indicate that the source is UTF-8, the Unicode character set discussed (https://www.learnenough.com/html-tutorial/html_intro#sec-an_html_skeleton) in *Learn Enough HTML to Be Dangerous* (https://www.learnenough.com/html).

The result of running this code is to load the full contents of the text file into the **text** variable:

```
> text.length;
1373
> text.split("\n")[0];       // Split on newlines and extract the 1st phrase.
'A butt tuba'
```

The second command here splits the text on the newline character **\n** and selects the zeroth element, revealing the enigmatic first line of the file, "A butt tuba".

Let's take the ideas from the REPL and put them in a script:

```
$ touch palindrome_file
$ chmod +x palindrome_file
```

The script itself is simple: We just open the file, split the contents on newlines, and iterate through the resulting array, printing any line that's a palindrome. The result, which at this stage you should aspire to read fairly easily, appears in Listing 10.1. (In this and subsequent examples, make sure that your shebang line matches the result of **which node** on your system if it differs from mine.)

Listing 10.1: Reading and processing the contents of a file.
palindrome_file

```
#!/usr/local/bin/node

let fs = require("fs");
let Phrase = require("<username>-palindrome");

let text = fs.readFileSync("phrases.txt", "utf-8");
text.split("\n").forEach(function(line) {
  let phrase = new Phrase(line);
  if (phrase.palindrome()) {
    console.log("palindrome detected:", line);
  }
});
```

Note that the code in Listing 10.1 will work only if the **palindrome** module was installed correctly (Section 9.1).

Running the script at the command line confirms that there are quite a few palindromes in the file:

```
$ ./palindrome_file
.
.
.
palindrome detected: Dennis sinned.
palindrome detected: Dennis and Edna sinned.
palindrome detected: Dennis, Nell, Edna, Leon, Nedra, Anita, Rolf, Nora,
Alice, Carol, Leo, Jane, Reed, Dena, Dale, Basil, Rae, Penny, Lana, Dave,
Denny, Lena, Ida, Bernadette, Ben, Ray, Lila, Nina, Jo, Ira, Mara, Sara,
Mario, Jan, Ina, Lily, Arne, Bette, Dan, Reba, Diane, Lynn, Ed, Eva, Dana,
Lynne, Pearl, Isabel, Ada, Ned, Dee, Rena, Joel, Lora, Cecil, Aaron, Flora,
Tina, Arden, Noel, and Ellen sinned.
palindrome detected: Go hang a salami, I'm a lasagna hog.
palindrome detected: level
palindrome detected: Madam, I'm Adam.
palindrome detected: No "x" in "Nixon"
palindrome detected: No devil lived on
palindrome detected: Race fast, safe car
palindrome detected: racecar
palindrome detected: radar
palindrome detected: Was it a bar or a bat I saw?
palindrome detected: Was it a car or a cat I saw?
palindrome detected: Was it a cat I saw?
palindrome detected: Yo, banana boy!
```

Among others, we see a rather elaborate expansion on the simple palindrome "Dennis sinned" (Figure 10.1)![1]

10.1.1 Exercise

1. Using whichever method you prefer (such as searching for node write file), add code to the script in Listing 10.1 to write all detected palindromes to a file called **palindromes.txt**.

10.2 Reading from URLs

In this section, we'll write a script whose effect is identical to the one in Section 10.1, except that it reads the **phrases.txt** file directly from its public URL. By itself,

---

1. Image courtesy of Historical Images Archive/Alamy Stock Photo.

Figure 10.1: Dennis, Nell, Edna, Leon, Nedra, and many others sinned.

the program doesn't do anything fancy, but realize what a miracle this is: The ideas aren't specific to the URL we're hitting, which means that after this section you'll have the power to write programs to access and process practically any public site on the Web. (This practice, sometimes called "web scraping", should be done with due consideration and caution.)

As in Section 10.1, installing an NPM module is a necessary prerequisite. As is often the case with NPM modules, there are multiple different ways to accomplish the same task. Based on the results of the web search node read web page url and a list of the alternatives to **request**,[2] we'll use the **urllib** module, which we can install as follows:[3]

```
$ npm install urllib
```

2. The original version of this tutorial used **request**, but it has since been deprecated.

3. For reasons I don't really understand, **urllib** module global installation doesn't work, at least on my system, so here we install it locally.

Then we can create our script as in Section 10.1:

```
$ touch palindrome_url
$ chmod +x palindrome_url
```

Consulting the **urllib** documentation (https://www.npmjs.com/package /urllib), we find (as of this writing) the example code in Listing 10.2.

Listing 10.2: Example code for reading the contents of a URL.

```
var urllib = require('urllib');

urllib.request('http://cnodejs.org/', function (err, data, res) {
  if (err) {
    throw err; // you need to handle error
  }
  console.log(res.statusCode);
  console.log(res.headers);
  // data is Buffer instance
  console.log(data.toString());
});
```

Bootstrapping off of code examples like Listing 10.2 is an excellent practice. Indeed, it's not a bad idea to actually execute the code at each stage, but for brevity I'll omit the output until the script is done.

We can modify the default code for our purposes by updating the conventions (such as using **let** in place of **var**), using more descriptive names, and eliminating lines that we definitely don't need:

```
let urllib = require("urllib");
urllib.request("http://www.cnodejs.org/", function(error, data, response) {
  console.log('body:', data.toString());
});
```

We begin to see the shape of a solution. The **urllib** module opens a web *request* for the given URL, and takes a function with three arguments: an error (if any), a data object containing the body of the page (which is the *full* page, not to be confused with the HTML **body** tag), and a response object.

It's important to emphasize at this point that *I don't know exactly what these objects are*, so you don't have to either. What I do know—what I can reasonably infer from the

Figure 10.2: Visiting the phrase URL.

example code in Listing 10.2—is that **data.toString()** is a string that can take the place of **text** in Listing 10.1. (Recall that we saw the **toString()** method applied to numbers in Section 4.1.2.) This is enough to solve our problem, because it means that we can replace the cnodejs.org URL in Listing 10.2 with the one for **phrases.txt**, and replace

```
console.log('body:', data.toString());
```

with the palindrome-detecting logic from Listing 10.1.

There's one final subtlety, which is that the URL for **phrases.txt** is actually a *redirect*: If you visit https://cdn.learnenough.com/phrases.txt, you'll find that in fact it *forwards* (using a 301 redirect) to a page on Amazon's Simple Storage Service (S3), as seen in Figure 10.2.

Some URL libraries follow redirects by default, but **urllib** does not, so we have to add an option (as described (https://www.npmjs.com/package/urllib#api-doc) in the **urllib** documentation):

```
urllib.request(url, { followRedirect: true }, function(error, data, response)
```

With the **followRedirect** option set to **true**, **urllib** will follow the 301 redirect to S3, so the final code appears as in Listing 10.3.

Listing 10.3: A URL-reading script.
palindrome_url

```
#!/usr/local/bin/node

let urllib = require("urllib");
let Phrase = require("mhartl-palindrome");
let url = 'https://cdn.learnenough.com/phrases.txt'

urllib.request(url, { followRedirect: true }, function(error, data, response) {
  let body = data.toString();
  body.split("\n").forEach(function(line) {
    let phrase = new Phrase(line);
    if (phrase.palindrome()) {
      console.log("palindrome detected:", line);
    }
  });
});
```

At this point, we're ready to try the script out at the command line:

```
$ ./palindrome_url
  .
  .
  .
palindrome detected: Dennis sinned.
palindrome detected: Dennis and Edna sinned.
palindrome detected: Dennis, Nell, Edna, Leon, Nedra, Anita, Rolf, Nora,
Alice, Carol, Leo, Jane, Reed, Dena, Dale, Basil, Rae, Penny, Lana, Dave,
Denny, Lena, Ida, Bernadette, Ben, Ray, Lila, Nina, Jo, Ira, Mara, Sara,
Mario, Jan, Ina, Lily, Arne, Bette, Dan, Reba, Diane, Lynn, Ed, Eva, Dana,
Lynne, Pearl, Isabel, Ada, Ned, Dee, Rena, Joel, Lora, Cecil, Aaron, Flora,
Tina, Arden, Noel, and Ellen sinned.
palindrome detected: Go hang a salami, I'm a lasagna hog.
palindrome detected: level
palindrome detected: Madam, I'm Adam.
```

```
palindrome detected: No "x" in "Nixon"
palindrome detected: No devil lived on
palindrome detected: Race fast, safe car
palindrome detected: racecar
palindrome detected: radar
palindrome detected: Was it a bar or a bat I saw?
palindrome detected: Was it a car or a cat I saw?
palindrome detected: Was it a cat I saw?
palindrome detected: Yo, banana boy!
```

Amazing! The result is exactly as we saw in Section 10.1, but this time, we got the data right off the live Web.

10.2.1 Exercise

1. It's often useful to have a separate variable with a list of the items you're selecting for (in this case, palindromes). Using the **filter** method discussed in Section 6.2, create a **palindromes** variable with an array of palindromes, as shown in Listing 10.4. Is the output the same as the output of Listing 10.3?

Listing 10.4: Reading a URL the functional way.
palindrome_url

```
#!/usr/local/bin/node

let urllib = require("urllib");
let Phrase = require("<username>-palindrome");
let url = 'https://cdn.learnenough.com/phrases.txt'

urllib.request(url, { followRedirect: true }, function(error, data, response) {
  let body  = data.toString();
  let lines = body.split("\n");
  let palindromes = lines.filter(line => /* FILL IN */);
  palindromes.forEach(function(palindrome) {
    console.log("palindrome detected:", palindrome);
  });
});
```

10.3 DOM Manipulation at the Command Line

In this final section, we're going to put the URL-reading tricks we learned in Section 10.2 to good use by writing a version of an actual utility script I once wrote for myself. To begin, I'll explain the context in which the script arose, and the problem it solves.

In recent years, there has been an explosion in the resources available for learning foreign languages, including things like Duolingo, Google Translate, and native OS support for multilingual text-to-speech (TTS). A few years ago, I decided to take advantage of this opportunity to brush up on my high-school/college Spanish.

One of the resources I found myself turning to was Wikipedia, with its huge number of articles in languages other than English. In particular, I discovered how useful it was to copy text from Spanish-language Wikipedia (Figure 10.3) and drop it into Google Translate (Figure 10.4). At that point, I could use the text-to-speech from either Google Translate (the red square in Figure 10.4) or macOS to hear the words spoken in Spanish, while following along with either the native language or the translation. Es muy útil.

After a while, I noticed two consistent sources of friction:

- Copying a large number of paragraphs by hand was cumbersome.

- Hand-copying text often selected things that I didn't want, particularly *reference numbers*, which the TTS system duly pronounced, resulting in random numbers in the middle of sentences (e.g., "Se define como orientado a objetos, 3 [tres] basado en prototipos" = "It's defined as object-oriented, 3 [three] based on prototypes." ¿Qué pasó?).

Friction like this has inspired many a utility script, and thus was born `wikp` ("Wikipedia paragraphs"), a program to download a Wikipedia article's HTML source, extract its paragraphs, and eliminate its reference numbers, dumping all the results to the screen.

The original `wikp` program was written in Ruby, but it's just as easy (and arguably easier) in JavaScript. We already know from Listing 10.3 how to download the source. The remaining tasks are then to:

1. Take an arbitrary URL argument at the command line.
2. Manipulate the downloaded HTML as if it were a regular DOM (Section 9.3).

Figure 10.3: Un artículo sobre JavaScript.

3. Remove the references.

4. Output the paragraphs.

I want to emphasize that, when I began writing this tutorial, *I couldn't do any of these things in JavaScript.* So this section isn't just about telling you how to do them; it's about teaching you how to figure these sorts of things out on your own—in other words, classic technical sophistication.

Let's get started by creating the initial script:

```
$ touch wikp
$ chmod +x wikp
```

Now we're ready to get going on the main program. For each task above, I'll include the kind of Google search you might use to figure out how to do it.

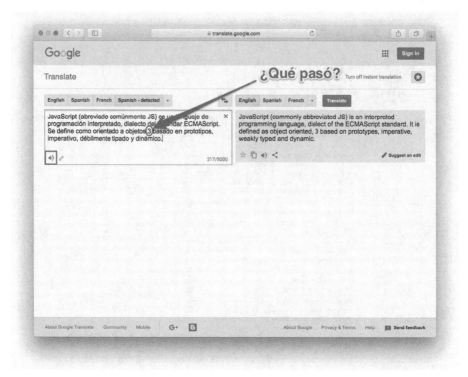

Figure 10.4: An article about JavaScript dropped into Google Translate.

First, we'll take in the URL as a command-line argument (javascript node command line arguments), as seen in Listing 10.5. Note that we've included a **console.log** line as a temporary way to track our progress.

Listing 10.5: Accept a command-line argument.
wikp

```
#!/usr/local/bin/node

// Returns the paragraphs from a Wikipedia link, stripped of reference numbers.

let urllib = require("urllib");
let url = process.argv[2];

console.log(url);
```

We can confirm that Listing 10.5 works as advertised:

```
$ ./wikp https://es.wikipedia.org/wiki/JavaScript
https://es.wikipedia.org/wiki/JavaScript
```

Next, we need to learn how to parse HTML with Node (node parse html), for which there are several possibilities. The one that connects best with what we already know is JSDOM:

```
$ npm install jsdom
```

Adding JSDOM to our script gives Listing 10.6.

Listing 10.6: Adding JSDOM.
wikp

```
#!/usr/local/bin/node

// Returns the paragraphs from a Wikipedia link, stripped of reference numbers.

let urllib = require("urllib");
let url = process.argv[2];
const jsdom = require("jsdom");
const { JSDOM } = jsdom;
```

Why does Listing 10.5 have this weird-looking assignment?

```
const { JSDOM } = jsdom;
```

The answer is, I don't know offhand; I copied-and-pasted the code directly from the JSDOM documentation (https://github.com/jsdom/jsdom#basic-usage). This is an essential skill for every developer (Figure 10.5).

We'll have to do a little more work to see the effects of JSDOM. Following the documentation, we see that we can create a simulated **document** object—just like the one we saw in Listing 9.8—using this code:

```
let { document } = (new JSDOM(body)).window;
```

Basic usage

```
const jsdom = require("jsdom");
const { JSDOM } = jsdom;
```

To use jsdom, you will primarily use the `JSDOM` constructor, which is a named export of the jsdom main module. Pass the constructor a string. You will get back a `JSDOM` object, which has a number of useful properties, notably `window` :

```
const dom = new JSDOM(`<!DOCTYPE html><p>Hello world</p>`);
console.log(dom.window.document.querySelector("p").textContent); // "Hello world"
```

(Note that jsdom will parse the HTML you pass it just like a browser does, including implied `<html>` , `<head>` , and `<body>` tags.)

The resulting object is an instance of the `JSDOM` class, which contains a number of useful properties and methods besides `window` . In general, it can be used to act on the jsdom from the "outside," doing things that are not possible with the normal DOM APIs. For simple cases, where you don't need any of this functionality, we recommend a coding pattern like

Figure 10.5: There's nothing wrong with a little copy-and-paste.

(The JSDOM documentation uses **const**, but we'll use **let** as a signal that we might change the document, which indeed we will (by removing references).)

Combining this with the download code from Listing 10.3 gives Listing 10.7.

Listing 10.7: Adding a simulated DOM.
wikp

```
#!/usr/local/bin/node

// Returns the paragraphs from a Wikipedia link, stripped of reference numbers.

let urllib = require("urllib");
let url = process.argv[2];
```

```
const jsdom = require("jsdom");
const { JSDOM } = jsdom;

urllib.request(url, { followRedirect: true }, function(error, data, response) {
  let body = data.toString();
  // Simulate a Document Object Model.
  let { document } = (new JSDOM(body)).window;
});
```

Our next task is to grab all the paragraphs and references. Since we have a simulated DOM, we can use something like the **querySelector** function we first saw in Section 9.2. That function returned only *one* DOM element, but we can guess how we might find them all (javascript queryselector return all elements). Indeed, as of this writing, the solution is the first example on the first Google hit:

```
let paragraphs = document.querySelectorAll("p");
```

(The only change I made was to modify **var matches** to read **let paragraphs**.)

Similar code applies to finding all the references, but here we need to know a little about Wikipedia's source. We can use the web inspector (Section 1.3.1) to see that the references all have CSS class **reference**, as shown in Figure 10.6.

Now, if I told you that the code

```
document.querySelector("#palindromeTester");
```

returned the element with CSS id **palindromeTester** (as in Listing 9.9), what would you guess is the code to find *all* the elements with CSS *class* equal to **reference**? The CSS notation for a class involves preceding it with a dot **.** instead of a #, and we just learned how to find them all using **querySelectorAll**, which means you can probably guess that it's this:

```
let references = document.querySelectorAll(".reference");
```

Adding these assignments to the script yields Listing 10.8.

Figure 10.6: Viewing a reference in the web inspector.

Listing 10.8: Pulling out the paragraphs and references.

wikp

```
#!/usr/local/bin/node

// Returns the paragraphs from a Wikipedia link, stripped of reference numbers.

let urllib = require("urllib");
let url = process.argv[2];

const jsdom = require("jsdom");
const { JSDOM } = jsdom;

urllib.request(url, { followRedirect: true }, function(error, data, response) {
  let body = data.toString();
  // Simulate a Document Object Model.
  let { document } = (new JSDOM(body)).window;
```

```
    // Grab all the paragraphs and references.
    let paragraphs = document.querySelectorAll("p");
    let references = document.querySelectorAll(".reference");
});
```

At this point, we're almost done. We just need to remove the references and then print out the contents of each paragraph. The first task is easy, as there's a native **remove** method to remove an HTML "node" (an element in the Document Object Model tree; javascript dom remove element):

```
references.forEach(function(reference) {
  reference.remove();
});
```

Note that this involves guessing that **references** is a collection that can be iterated through using **forEach**, which at this point should be within your powers of technical sophistication. (Technically, **querySelectorAll** returns not an array, but rather a "NodeList". Nevertheless, this object can be traversed using **forEach** just the same.)

The second task is also simple once we know that each element has a **textContent** property (javascript dom element print content):

```
paragraphs.forEach(function(paragraph) {
  console.log(paragraph.textContent);
});
```

Putting everything together gives the **wikp** script shown in Listing 10.9.

Listing 10.9: The final Wikipedia paragraph script.
wikp

```
#!/usr/local/bin/node

// Returns the paragraphs from a Wikipedia link, stripped of reference numbers.

let urllib = require("urllib");
let url = process.argv[2];

const jsdom = require("jsdom");
const { JSDOM } = jsdom;

urllib.request(url, { followRedirect: true }, function(error, data, response) {
```

```
let body = data.toString();
// Simulate a Document Object Model.
let { document } = (new JSDOM(body)).window;

// Grab all the paragraphs and references.
let paragraphs = document.querySelectorAll("p");
let references = document.querySelectorAll(".reference");

// Remove any references.
references.forEach(function(reference) {
   reference.remove();
});
// Print out all of the paragraphs.
paragraphs.forEach(function(paragraph) {
   console.log(paragraph.textContent);
});
});
```

Let's see how things went:

```
$ ./wikp https://es.wikipedia.org/wiki/JavaScript
.
.
.
Existen algunas herramientas de ayuda a la depuración, también escritas en
JavaScript y construidas para ejecutarse en la Web. Un ejemplo es el programa
JSLint, desarrollado por Douglas Crockford, quien ha escrito extensamente
sobre el lenguaje. JSLint analiza el código JavaScript para que este quede
conforme con un conjunto de normas y directrices y que aseguran su correcto
funcionamiento y mantenibilidad.
```

Success! By scrolling up in our terminal, we can now select all the text and drop it
into Google Translate or a text editor of our choice. On macOS, we can do even
better by piping (https://www.learnenough.com/command-line-tutorial/inspecting
_files#sec-wordcount_and_pipes) the results to **pbcopy**, which automatically copies
the results to the macOS **p**aste**b**oard (also called the "clipboard"):

```
$ ./wikp https://es.wikipedia.org/wiki/JavaScript | pbcopy
```

At this point, pasting into Google Translate (or anywhere else) will paste the full text.[4]

---

4. Google Translate has a limit for how much text it will translate at once, but for text-to-speech purposes
you can always paste into a word processor and then use the operating system's native TTS functionality.

Consider how remarkable this accomplishment is. The script in Listing 10.9 is a little tricky—and to get such a thing working completely on your own might involve more than a few **console.log** statements as you go along—but it's not exactly rocket science. And yet, it's genuinely useful, something that (if you're active in foreign-language learning) you might well use all the time. Moreover, the basic skills involved—including not just the programming, but also the technical sophistication (<cough>Googling</cough>)—unlock a huge number of potential applications.

10.3.1 Exercises

1. By moving the file or changing your system's configuration, add the **wikp** script to your environment's PATH. (You may find the steps (https://www .learnenough.com/text-editor-tutorial/advanced_text_editing#sec-writing_an_ executable_script) in *Learn Enough Text Editor to Be Dangerous* (https://www .learnenough.com/text-editor) helpful.) Confirm that you can run **wikp** without prepending **./** to the command name.

2. What happens if you run **wikp** with no argument? Add code to your script to detect the absence of a command-line argument and output an appropriate usage statement. *Hint*: After printing out the usage statement, you will have to *exit*, which you can learn how to do with the search "node how to exit script".

3. The "pipe to **pbcopy**" trick mentioned in the text works only on macOS, but any Unix-compatible system can redirect (https://www.learnenough.com/command -line-tutorial/manipulating_files#sec-redirecting_and_appending) the output to a file. What's the command to redirect the output of **wikp** to a file called **article.txt**? (You could then open this file, select all, and copy the contents, which has the same basic result as piping to **pbcopy**.)

CHAPTER 11

Full Sample App: Image Gallery

As a final application of our newfound JavaScript powers, in this last chapter we'll build on the sample application developed in *Learn Enough CSS & Layout to Be Dangerous* (https://www.learnenough.com/css-and-layout). (We'll be *cloning* the initial sample repository, so you'll be able to complete this chapter even if you didn't follow the CSS tutorial.) In particular, we'll follow a time-honored tradition in JavaScript tutorials and create an *image gallery*, which will allow us to display and swap custom images—in our case, a fancy three-column layout (https://www.learnenough.com/css-and-layout-tutorial/flex-intro#sec-pages-3col).

After prepping the gallery (Section 11.1), we'll learn how to change the gallery image (Section 11.2), set an image as "current" (Section 11.3), and change the image title and description (Section 11.4). Because our starting point is the professional-grade website developed in *Learn Enough CSS & Layout to Be Dangerous*, the result is unusually polished for a JavaScript tutorial sample gallery (Figure 11.1).

11.1 Prepping the Gallery

To get started with our image gallery, you'll need to get a copy of the full starting application (https://github.com/learnenough/le_js_full) for the site. The first step is to make a personal copy of the app, which you can do using the *fork* capability at GitHub (Figure 11.2).

The next step depends on whether or not you currently have a GitHub Pages site at <username>.github.io. If you don't have such a repository, you can rename

Figure 11.1: This is the gallery we're looking for.

your app accordingly (Figure 11.3), and it will automatically be available at the URL
<username>.github.io.

Once you've renamed the repo, you can clone the gallery app to your local system
using the clone URL from GitHub (Figure 11.4):

```
$ git clone <clone URL> <username>.github.io
```

If you already have a repository at <username>.github.io from following *Learn
Enough CSS & Layout to Be Dangerous*, you should clone the gallery app (without
renaming it) to the default directory by omitting the second argument to **git clone**:

```
$ git clone <clone URL>     # Command if you already have <username>.github.io
```

This will create a local repository called **le_js_full**, which you can use as a reference
for copying over the required files. In particular, you'll need the gallery **index.html**
and the large and small images:

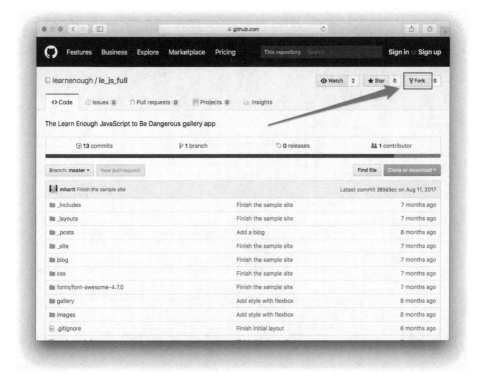

Figure 11.2: Forking the starting application at GitHub.

```
# Run these commands only if you already have <username>.github.io
# from following Learn Enough CSS & Layout to Be Dangerous.
$ cd le_js_full/
$ cp gallery/index.html /path/to/repo/<username>.github.io/gallery/
$ cp -r images/* /path/to/repo/<username>.github.io/images/
```

(If you already have a repo at <username>.github.io that *isn't* the result of following *Learn Enough CSS & Layout to Be Dangerous*, I'll assume you have the requisite technical sophistication to figure something out on your own.)

In either case, once the app is put together you can run it using the Jekyll static site builder. The Jekyll setup instructions (https://www.learnenough.com/css-and-layout-tutorial/struct-layout#sec-jekyll) in *Learn Enough CSS & Layout to Be Dangerous* explain how to install Jekyll on your system in case it isn't installed already. The short version is that you first need to install *Bundler*:

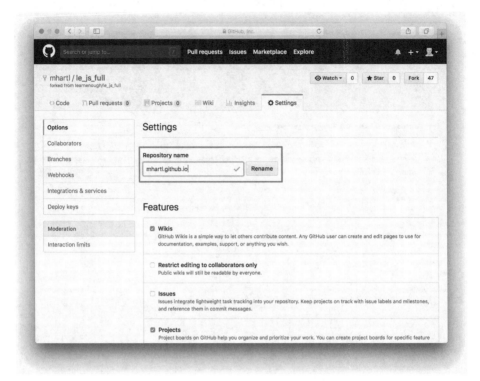

Figure 11.3: Renaming to the default GitHub Pages name.

```
$ gem install bundler -v 2.2.17
```

Then use the **bundle** command to install the **jekyll** gem listed in the **Gemfile** included with the repository:

```
$ bundle _2.2.17_ install
```

Once Jekyll is installed, you can serve the sample website by using Bundler to execute the correct version of the **jekyll** program:

```
$ bundle exec jekyll serve
```

At this point, the app will be running on localhost:4000, and should look something like Figure 11.5.

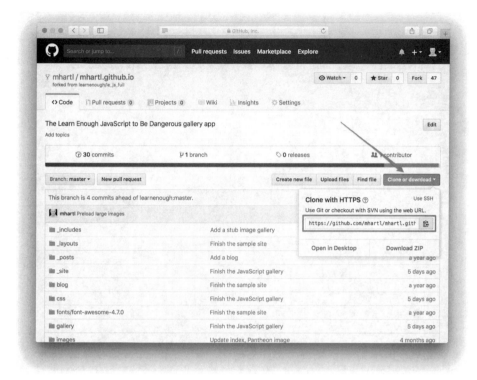

Figure 11.4: Getting the clone URL at GitHub.

11.1.1   Prepping the JavaScript

As a final bit of prep, we'll add a stub for the main gallery function, **activateGallery**, which we'll be filling in throughout the rest of this chapter. Because we'll be doing everything in plain JavaScript, there will be no need to include any Node modules, run **browserify**, etc. In fact, all we'll need to do is write a single function.

Our first step is to make a directory and JavaScript file (remember, this is in the app directory, not **js_tutorial**):

```
$ mkdir js
$ touch js/gallery.js
```

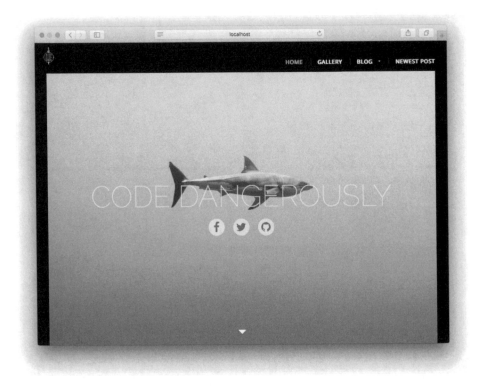

Figure 11.5: Our initial sample app.

Just to get started, we'll add an initial alert to **gallery.js** (Listing 11.1).

Listing 11.1: A stub gallery file.

js/gallery.js

```
function activateGallery() {
  alert("Hello from the gallery file!");
}
```

In the head of the file, we'll include the gallery JavaScript using the **src** attribute (Section 5.2), and add an event listener (Section 9.2) to run the gallery activation function automatically after the DOM is loaded (Listing 9.9). The result appears in Listing 11.2.

Listing 11.2: Including the gallery JavaScript.
_includes/head.html

```
<head>
  .
  .
  .
  <link rel="stylesheet" href="/css/main.css">

  <script src="/js/gallery.js"></script>
  <script>
    document.addEventListener("DOMContentLoaded", function() {
      activateGallery();
    });
  </script>
</head>
```

Now visiting the local gallery page confirms that the JavaScript was loaded correctly (Figure 11.6).

11.1.2 Exercise

1. Deploy your stub gallery to GitHub Pages and confirm that it works in production.

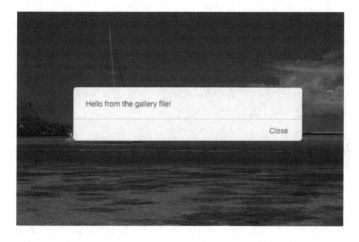

Hello from the gallery file!

Close

Figure 11.6: Hello from the gallery!

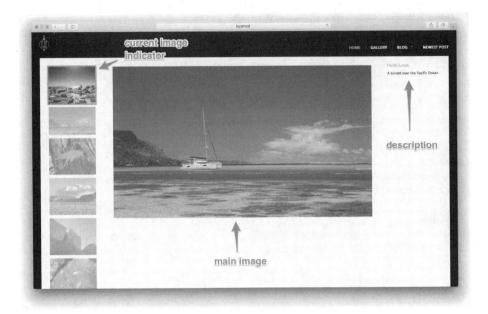

Figure 11.7: The initial gallery.

11.2 Changing the Gallery Image

Let's take a look at the current state of the application. The gallery page has three columns: one with smaller "thumbnail" images, one with the main image, and one with the description. As seen in Figure 11.7, in the default state the "current image" indicator in the thumbnails doesn't match the main image, and the description doesn't match either.

We can see the origins of this mismatch by taking a look at the current HTML structure of the gallery, which appears as in Listing 11.3.

Listing 11.3: The gallery HTML.
gallery/index.html

```
1   ---
2   layout: default
3   title: Gallery for Learn Enough JavaScript to Be Dangerous
4   ---
5
6   <div class="gallery col-three">
```

```
 7   <div class="col col-nav gallery-thumbs" id="gallery-thumbs">
 8     <div class="current">
 9       <img src="/images/small/beach.jpg" alt="Venice Beach"
10             data-large-version="/images/large/beach.jpg"
11             data-title="Venice Beach"
12             data-description="An overhead shot of Venice Beach, California.">
13     </div>
14     .
15     .
16     .
17     <div>
18       <img src="/images/small/turtle.jpg" alt="turtle"
19             data-large-version="/images/large/turtle.jpg"
20             data-title="Sea Turtle"
21             data-description="A friendly sea turtle.">
22     </div>
23   </div>
24   <div class="col col-content">
25     <div class="gallery-photo" id="gallery-photo">
26       <img src="/images/large/boat.jpg" alt="Catamaran">
27     </div>
28   </div>
29   <div class="col col-aside gallery-info" id="gallery-info">
30     <h3 class="title">Pacific Sunset</h3>
31     <p class="description">A sunset over the Pacific Ocean.</p>
32   </div>
33 </div>
```

From Listing 11.3, we see that the current image is indicated with a CSS class **current** (Line 8), the main image is in an HTML **div** with CSS id **gallery-photo** (Line 25), and the title and description are in a div with CSS id **gallery-info** (Line 29). Our task is to dynamically update this HTML (Section 9.3) so that all three columns match.

Our first task is the biggest one in terms of the user interface, namely, swapping out the main image when the user clicks on a thumbnail. Our strategy is to put an event listener (Section 9.2) on each image, and then change the source (**src**) of the main display image on click.

To do this, we'll first create a variable with a list of all the images.[1] Inspecting the HTML source in Listing 11.3, we see that the thumbnail images are all **img** tags inside

---

1. As noted briefly in Section 10.3, technically the result of **querySelectorAll** is a "NodeList" object, not an array, but we can treat it as an array for the purposes of iteration. Specifically, we can traverse its elements using the **forEach** method.

a **div** with CSS id **gallery-thumbs**. As a result, we can select all the thumbnails using method chaining (Section 5.3) by combining **querySelector** (Section 9.2) to select the thumbnail div and **querySelectorAll** (Section 10.3) to select all the images:

```
let thumbnails = document.querySelector("#gallery-thumbs").
                          querySelectorAll("img");
```

Note that JavaScript allows us to break method calls across lines in order to make the structure clearer and avoid breaking the 80-character limit (Box 2.3).

By iterating through the collection of **thumbnails**, we can put an event listener on each one using code like this:

```
thumbnails.forEach(function(thumbnail) {
  thumbnail.addEventListener("click", function() {
    // code to set clicked image as main image
  });
});
```

This arranges to listen for the same "click" event we saw in Listing 9.13.

As indicated in the JavaScript comment in the middle of the code sample, the body of the listener should set the clicked image as the main image. The way we'll do this is to set the **src** attribute of the current display image to the "large" version of the image clicked. Referring to Listing 11.3, we see that the main image is inside a **div** with CSS id **gallery-photo**, so we can select it by chaining **querySelector**:

```
let mainImage = document.querySelector("#gallery-photo").
                         querySelector("img");
```

In fact, **querySelector** is smart enough to let us combine this into a single command:

```
let mainImage = document.querySelector("#gallery-photo img");
```

It's worth noting that there's an equivalent alternate notation that uses an angle bracket **>** to emphasize the nesting relationship between the elements (in this case, an **img** element nested inside an element with CSS id **gallery-photo**):

```
let mainImage = document.querySelector("#gallery-photo > img");
```

We'll use this alternate notation with **querySelectorAll** in Section 11.2.1.

Once we have the main image, we can use the **setAttribute** method (javascript dom set attribute src) to change its **src** attribute:

```
mainImage.setAttribute("src", newImageSrc);
```

If you've been following along closely, you're now aware that everything we need has been created except for **newImageSrc**, the source of the new image. Happily, the sample app has already arranged to encode the necessary path in the image tag itself. Suppose for the sake of argument that we clicked on the Pacific sunset image, whose HTML looks like this:

```
<div>
  <img src="/images/small/sunset.jpg" alt="sunset"
       data-large-version="/images/large/sunset.jpg"
       data-title="Pacific Sunset"
       data-description="A sunset over the Pacific Ocean.">
</div>
```

Encoding data in a tag like this is an essential aspect of *unobtrusive JavaScript*, which involves never putting JavaScript in the body of the HTML itself. When using these data attributes on HTML tags, the browser automatically creates a special **dataset** attribute, whose values correspond to the HTML source as follows:

```
data-large-version -> thumbnail.dataset.largeVersion
data-title         -> thumbnail.dataset.title
data-description   -> thumbnail.dataset.description
```

In general, the data tag **data-foo-bar-baz** on HTML element **object** corresponds to the variable **object.dataset.fooBarBaz**, where the final attribute is in CamelCase (Figure 2.3).

We now have everything we need to replace the main image with the clicked image. If you'd like to give it a go on your own, it makes for an excellent exercise. As usual, use the debugging console (Box 5.1) if you run into trouble. The answer appears in Listing 11.4.

Listing 11.4: Setting the main gallery image.
js/gallery.js

```
// Activates the image gallery.
// The main task is to attach an event listener to each image in the gallery
// and respond appropriately on click.
```

```
function activateGallery() {
  let thumbnails = document.querySelector("#gallery-thumbs").
                              querySelectorAll("img");
  let mainImage = document.querySelector("#gallery-photo img");

  thumbnails.forEach(function(thumbnail) {
    thumbnail.addEventListener("click", function() {
      // Set clicked image as main image.
      let newImageSrc = thumbnail.dataset.largeVersion;
      mainImage.setAttribute("src", newImageSrc);
    });
  });
}
```

In addition to changing the **src** attribute, we should also change the **alt** attribute of the swapped-in image. Adding this detail is left as an exercise (Section 11.2.1).

Scrolling down and clicking on the Pacific sunset image produces the expected result (Figure 11.8). The agreement with the third-column description, however, is a coincidence, which can be seen by clicking on any other image (Figure 11.9). In addition, the orange "current image" indicator matches the main image in the gallery only if we happen to click on the corresponding thumbnail (Figure 11.10).

11.2.1 Exercises

1. The code in Listing 11.4 swaps in the **src** of the new large image, but unfortunately the **alt** attribute is still the default one from Listing 11.3 (Figure 11.11). Remedy this minor blemish in Listing 11.5 by replacing **FILL_IN** with the proper value. *Hint*: The value of the image **src** for **thumbnail** is given by **thumbnail.src**, so how do you suppose you get the value of **thumbnail**'s **alt** attribute?

2. As hinted in the main text, it's possible to change the **thumbnails** definition in Listing 11.4 to eliminate method chaining. We begin by noting that the gallery thumbnails are **img** tags inside **div** tags inside an element with CSS id **gallery-thumbs**; conveniently, we can indicate "inside" using the right angle bracket **>**. By replacing **???** in Listing 11.6 with the appropriate tags, show that we can condense the definition of **thumbnails** down to a single line. *Note*: I generally recommend choosing one convention and sticking with it, but for now we'll leave the arguments of **querySelectorAll** and **querySelector** inconsistent (one with angle brackets, one without) to emphasize that either notation works.

Figure 11.8: A Pacific sunset.

Listing 11.5: Updating the image `alt` attribute.
js/gallery.js

```
// Activates the image gallery.
// The main task is to attach an event listener to each image in the gallery
// and respond appropriately on click.
function activateGallery() {
  let thumbnails = document.querySelector("#gallery-thumbs").
                            querySelectorAll("img");
  let mainImage = document.querySelector("#gallery-photo img");

  thumbnails.forEach(function(thumbnail) {
    thumbnail.addEventListener("click", function() {
      // Set clicked image as main image.
      let newImageSrc = thumbnail.dataset.largeVersion;
      mainImage.setAttribute("src", newImageSrc);
      mainImage.setAttribute("alt", FILL_IN);
    });
  });
}
```

Figure 11.9: The image/description match in Figure 11.8 was a coincidence.

Figure 11.10: The "current image" match here is also a coincidence.

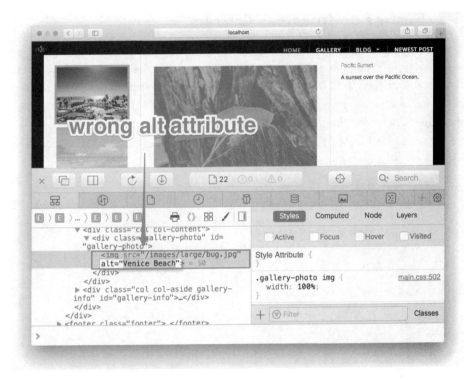

Figure 11.11: The `alt` attribute doesn't match the image `src`.

Listing 11.6: Condensing `thumbnails` into a single line.
js/gallery.js

```
// Activates the image gallery.
// The main task is to attach an event listener to each image in the gallery
// and respond appropriately on click.
function activateGallery() {
  let thumbnails = document.querySelectorAll("#gallery-thumbs > ??? > ???");
  let mainImage  = document.querySelector("#gallery-photo img");
  .
  .
  .
}
```

11.3 Setting an Image as Current

Section 11.2 represents a major accomplishment: The main task of a photo gallery—namely, swapping the main display image based on a user's click—is done. All we need to do now is change the "current image" indicator in the first column (this section) and update the image info in the third column (Section 11.4). Both tasks involve a mix of new and old techniques.

As seen in Listing 11.3, the current image is indicated in the HTML source using a CSS class called **current**:

```
<div class="current">
  <img src="/images/small/beach.jpg" alt="Venice Beach"
      data-large-version="/images/large/beach.jpg"
      data-title="Venice Beach"
      data-description="An overhead shot of Venice Beach, California.">
</div>
```

This arranges for an orange box shadow due to a line in **main.css**:

```
.
.
.
.gallery-thumbs .current img {
  box-shadow: 0 0 0 5px #ed6e2f;
  opacity: 1;
}
.
.
.
```

Our basic strategy is to add code to the listener in Listing 11.4 that arranges to remove the current image indicator from the thumbnail it's on and move it to the thumbnail that's been clicked. This is a little trickier than it looks because the class isn't on the image—it's on the **div** *surrounding* the image. Luckily, JavaScript lets us navigate up and down the DOM with ease, so that we can easily access the DOM element one level up in the tree (Figure 9.6)—the so-called *parent node*.

In short, our algorithm for changing the current image class is as follows:

1. Find the current thumbnail and remove the **current** class.
2. Add the **current** class to the *parent* of the clicked image.

Because there's only one element on the page with class **current**, we can select it using **querySelector**:

```
document.querySelector(".current");
```

But how can we remove the class? Ah: javascript dom remove class. This leads us to the **classList** method and its attendant **remove** method:

```
document.querySelector(".current").classList.remove("current");
```

There's a lot of method chaining here, but its meaning is clear enough.

Happily, once we know how to find the parent node of an element (javascript dom parent node), we can use the corresponding **classList.add** method (javascript dom add class) to add the desired class:

```
thumbnail.parentNode.classList.add("current");
```

Putting these together means we're already done! The result appears in Listing 11.7 (which includes the result of solving the exercise in Section 11.2.1).

Listing 11.7: Changing the current class.
js/gallery.js

```
// Activates the image gallery.
// The main task is to attach an event listener to each image in the gallery
// and respond appropriately on click.
function activateGallery() {
  let thumbnails = document.querySelectorAll("#gallery-thumbs > div > img");
  let mainImage  = document.querySelector("#gallery-photo img");

  thumbnails.forEach(function(thumbnail) {
    thumbnail.addEventListener("click", function() {
      // Set clicked image as display image.
      let newImageSrc = thumbnail.dataset.largeVersion;
      mainImage.setAttribute("src", newImageSrc);

      // Change which image is current.
      document.querySelector(".current").classList.remove("current");
      thumbnail.parentNode.classList.add("current");
    });
  });
}
```

Figure 11.12: Mammoth Mountain.

As a result of the code in Listing 11.7, clicking on a thumbnail automatically updates the current image indicator, whether the image is Mammoth Mountain in the Sierras (Figure 11.12) or The Huntington in San Marino, California (Figure 11.13).

11.3.1 Exercise

1. There's a little duplication in Listing 11.7; in particular, it repeats the string literal **"current"**. Eliminate this duplication by factoring the string into a variable called **currentClass**.

11.4 Changing the Image Info

Our final task is to update the image information (title and description) in the third column of our gallery. Doing this doesn't actually require anything we haven't seen before—we just have to put things we already know together in a slightly new way, making this an excellent way to end the tutorial.

Figure 11.13: The Chinese Garden at The Huntington.

The sequence we'll follow is simple:

1. Find the DOM elements for the image title and description.
2. Replace the contents with the corresponding data from the clicked image.

To find the necessary DOM elements, we first observe that they are both inside the **div** with CSS id **gallery-info**:

```
<div class="col col-aside gallery-info" id="gallery-info">

  <h3 class="title">Pacific Sunset</h3>
  <p class="description">A sunset over the Pacific Ocean.</p>
</div>
```

Inside that **div**, both are the first (and only) elements with the **title** and **description** classes, respectively, which means we can select them as follows:

```
let galleryInfo = document.querySelector("#gallery-info");
let title       = galleryInfo.querySelector(".title");
let description = galleryInfo.querySelector(".description");
```

Note that I've added extra spaces to line up the equals signs, which is a nice (though not strictly necessary) code formatting practice (Box 2.3).

We can get the corresponding values for the clicked image using the **dataset** variable introduced in Section 11.2:

```
thumbnail.dataset.title
```

for the title and

```
thumbnail.dataset.description
```

for the description.

The final piece of the puzzle is the **innerHTML** property we first saw in Section 9.3, which lets us directly update the inner HTML of a DOM element:

```
title.innerHTML       = thumbnail.dataset.title;
description.innerHTML = thumbnail.dataset.description;
```

Putting everything together gives the final version of the **activateGallery** function, shown in Listing 11.8.

Listing 11.8: Updating the image title and description on click.
js/gallery.js

```
// Activates the image gallery.
// The main task is to attach an event listener to each image in the gallery
// and respond appropriately on click.
function activateGallery() {
  let thumbnails = document.querySelectorAll("#gallery-thumbs > div > img");
  let mainImage  = document.querySelector("#gallery-photo img");
  // Image info to be updated
  let galleryInfo = document.querySelector("#gallery-info");
  let title       = galleryInfo.querySelector(".title");
  let description = galleryInfo.querySelector(".description");

  thumbnails.forEach(function(thumbnail) {
    thumbnail.addEventListener("click", function() {
      // Set clicked image as display image.
      let newImageSrc = thumbnail.dataset.largeVersion;
      mainImage.setAttribute("src", newImageSrc);
```

```
    // Change which image is current.
    document.querySelector(".current").classList.remove("current");
    thumbnail.parentNode.classList.add("current");

    // Update image info.
    title.innerHTML       = thumbnail.dataset.title;
    description.innerHTML = thumbnail.dataset.description;
  });
 });
}
```

Our final change involves syncing up the three columns for new visitors, so that the first column (current image indicator), second column (main image), and third column (image information) all match. This just involves updating the gallery index HTML as in Listing 11.9.

Listing 11.9: All three columns synced.
gallery/index.html

```
---
layout: default
title: Gallery for Learn Enough JavaScript to Be Dangerous
---

<div class="gallery col-three">
  <div class="col col-nav gallery-thumbs" id="gallery-thumbs">
    <div class="current">
      <img src="/images/small/beach.jpg" alt="Venice Beach"
          data-large-version="/images/large/beach.jpg"
          data-title="Venice Beach"
          data-description="An overhead shot of Venice Beach, California.">
    </div>
    .
    .
    .
  </div>
  <div class="col col-content">
    <div class="gallery-photo" id="gallery-photo">
      <img src="/images/large/beach.jpg" alt="Venice Beach">
    </div>
  </div>
  <div class="col col-aside gallery-info" id="gallery-info">
    <h3 class="title">Venice Beach</h3>
    <p class="description">An overhead shot of Venice Beach, California.</p>
  </div>
</div>
```

Figure 11.14: An overhead shot of Venice Beach, California.

Now all three of our columns agree, whether it's the Venice Beach pic that greets new visitors (Figure 11.14), a friendly sea turtle (Figure 11.15), Walt Disney Concert Hall in downtown Los Angeles (Figure 11.16), or the Flavian Amphitheater (Colosseum) in Rome (Figure 11.17).

11.4.1 Deploying

Because all the necessary files—including all the JavaScript—are completely local to our project (unlike some of the NPM modules in previous chapters), we can deploy our app to GitHub Pages with a simple **git push**:

```
$ git add -A
$ git commit -m "Finish the JavaScript gallery"
$ git push
```

Visiting the gallery at <username>.github.io and clicking on an image confirms it: We've deployed our dynamic JavaScript application to the live Web (Figure 11.18)!

Figure 11.15: A friendly sea turtle.

(To learn how to host a GitHub Pages site using a custom domain instead of a github.io subdomain, see the free tutorial *Learn Enough Custom Domains to Be Dangerous* (https://www.learnenough.com/custom-domains).)

11.4.2 Exercise

1. When clicking on a new thumbnail image on the live site (Figure 11.18), you might notice a slight delay before the main image appears in the center. This is because, unlike the thumbnails, the large versions haven't been downloaded yet.

   It's a common practice to prevent this small but annoying delay by *preloading* the images in the background to put them into the browser cache—a task we can accomplish with JavaScript. The trick is to create a new **Image** object (javascript image object) and assign it the **src** of the large image corresponding to each thumbnail. This forces the browser to download *all* the large images before the page is even loaded.

   By filling in the code in Listing 11.10 and deploying the result, confirm that image preloading works, and that the resulting image swapping is snappy and

Figure 11.16: Walt Disney Concert Hall in downtown Los Angeles.

responsive. (Note that we've hoisted **newImageSrc** out of the listener, which is a big hint about what to use to replace **FILL_IN**.)

Listing 11.10: Preloading large versions.
js/gallery.js

```
// Activates the image gallery.
// The main task is to attach an event listener to each image in the gallery
// and respond appropriately on click.
function activateGallery() {
  let thumbnails = document.querySelectorAll("#gallery-thumbs > div > img");
  let mainImage  = document.querySelector("#gallery-photo img");

  thumbnails.forEach(function(thumbnail) {
    // Preload large images.
    let newImageSrc  = thumbnail.dataset.largeVersion;
    let largeVersion = new Image();
    largeVersion.src = FILL_IN;
    thumbnail.addEventListener("click", function() {
      // Set clicked image as display image.
```

```
      mainImage.setAttribute("src", newImageSrc);

      // Change which image is current.
      document.querySelector(".current").classList.remove("current");
      thumbnail.parentNode.classList.add("current");

      // Update image info.
      let galleryInfo = document.querySelector("#gallery-info");
      let title       = galleryInfo.querySelector(".title");
      let description = galleryInfo.querySelector(".description");

      title.innerHTML       = thumbnail.dataset.title;
      description.innerHTML = thumbnail.dataset.description;
    });
  });
}
```

11.5 Conclusion

Congratulations! You now know enough JavaScript to be *dangerous*.

Figure 11.17: The Flavian Amphitheater (Colosseum) in Rome.

Figure 11.18: Our JavaScript gallery app on the live Web.

With the skills developed in this tutorial, you now have the preparation to go in multiple different directions. There are two in particular that I recommend. These are (1) learning more JavaScript and (2) making sure JavaScript isn't the only language you know.

11.5.1 Learning More JavaScript

There are approximately ∞ resources for learning more about JavaScript. Now that you know the basics, one good thing to focus on is expanding your command of the language syntax, as well as learning more advanced techniques (such as *async/await* and *promises*) and continuing to develop real applications. Here are a few resources that I've used or that have come highly recommended:

- Codecademy JavaScript (https://www.codecademy.com/learn/introduction-to-javascript): A guided in-browser introduction to JavaScript that's highly complementary to the approach in *Learn Enough JavaScript to Be Dangerous*.

- Treehouse JavaScript (https://teamtreehouse.com/library/topic:javascript): Well-regarded interactive tutorials.

- Wes Bos JavaScript (https://javascript30.com/): A free course on vanilla JavaScript. Wes also offers a large number of premium courses (https://wesbos.com/courses), many of them focused on JavaScript topics like ES6 and Node.

- Learn JavaScript Essentials (https://medium.com/javascript-scene/learn-javascript-b631a4af11f2#.lsb25e2f5): An excellent list of resources compiled by Eric Elliott (https://medium.com/@_ericelliott), including links to additional courses and books.

11.5.2 Learning a New Language

Ask experienced devs if it's important to know more than one programming language, and the answers will typically range from "yes!" to "extremely, indubitably yes!" Indeed, there are many reasons not to become a monoglot.

When it comes to building software for the greatest platform ever—the World Wide Web—the language I recommend (other than JavaScript) is *Ruby*, a powerful language designed for "programmer happiness". In particular, Ruby is the language of two of the most popular frameworks for making web applications, *Sinatra* (used at companies like Disney and Stripe) and *Rails* (used at companies like GitHub, Hulu, and Airbnb).

Though suitable for bigger applications, Sinatra is the simpler framework, and is included as part of *Learn Enough Ruby to Be Dangerous* (https://www.learnenough.com/ruby). Rails is my preferred framework for making database-backed web applications, and is thoroughly covered by the *Ruby on Rails Tutorial* (https://railstutorial.org/book). Moreover, both can be used with JavaScript, with Rails/JavaScript integration being especially popular.

As a result, these are the recommended continuations of the *Learn Enough* sequence:

- *Learn Enough Ruby to Be Dangerous*
- *Ruby on Rails Tutorial*

Finally, for people who want the most solid foundation possible in technical sophistication, Learn Enough All Access (https://www.learnenough.com/all-access) is a subscription service that has special online versions of all the Learn Enough books and over 40 hours of streaming video tutorials. We hope you'll check it out!

Index

Symbols

\ (backslash), 75
" (double quotes), 25–29
[] (bracket) notation, 56
!! (bang bang), 43–44
' (single quote), 25
{} (curly braces), 32, 37
(hash symbol), 195
% (modulo operator), 124
/ (slash character), 28–29
! operator, 42, 43
&& operator, 40, 41
+ operator, 27
|| operator, 41

A

accessing
  arrays, 56–58
  combining arrays, 63
  DOM (Document Object Model), 250
  string characters, 50
accumulators, 127
activating tools, 16
adding
  buttons, 193
  comments, 28–29
  event listeners, 195
  forms, 201, 207, 208
  HTML forms, 201
  notifications, 203
  pending tests, 162–163
  proof of concept, 187, 188
  stubs, 170
  testing, 169
alerts, 4, 34
alt attributes, updating, 247
anonymous functions, 110, 118, 196
applications
  code, 165 (*see also* code)
  deploying, 10–13
  functions from external files, 102
  image gallery (sample application), 235
    (*see also* image gallery)
  testing, 153
applying
  calculators, 66
  native assertions, 169
  REPLs (Read-Evaluate-Print Loops), 100
  technical sophistication, 28
  triple equals, 36
arguments, 22
  command-line, 226
  functions, 92, 93 (*see also* functions)
arrays, 55
  accessing, 56–58
  associative, 81
  creating URL-appropriate strings for, 118
  filter method, 122–125

iteration, 62–64, 111, 112
methods, 59–62
popping, 61
pushing, 61
reversing, 60
slicing, 58–59
sorting, 60
sorting numerical, 92–94
splitting, 55–56
undoing splits, 61–62
asserting
    applying active assertions, 169
    equality, 168
assigning
    properties, 135
    variables, 29, 31
associative arrays, 81
attributes, 35. *See also* string properties
    src, 100
automated tests, 132, 153, 159–164. *See also*
    testing
auxiliary functions, 120, 121

B

backslash (\\), 75
backtick syntax, 31–32
bang bang (!!), 43–44
Bash (Bourne-again shell), 6
block structures, 38
Boole, George, 367
booleans
    combining/inverting, 40–43
    strings, 35–44
Bourne-again shell. *See* Bash
bracket ([]), notation, 56
browserify utility, 188, 189, 191
browsers. *See also* viewing
    compatibility, 5
    consoles, 14–19, 99
    developer tools, 17
    JavaScript in, 7–14
    languages for, 1
bugfixes, 157
bugs, 166. *See also* errors; troubleshooting
built-in objects, 3

bundle command, 238
bundles, 189
buttons
    adding, 193
    wild, 194
button tag, 192, 193, 206

C

calculators, applying, 66
calls, functions, 9
CamelCase, 136
cascading style sheet. *See* CSS (cascading
    style sheet)
chains
    methods, 104–110, 180
    prototypes, 139
changes, committing to, 11. *See also* modifying
characters
    iteration, 50
    pushing, 173
    string literals, 25 (*see also* strings)
charAt method, 52, 53, 173
chmod command, 23
classes
    current, 250, 251
    equivalence, 124
cloning, 235
code. *See also* applications
    applications, 165
    DRY principle, 142
    event listeners, 196
    formatting, 38–39
    palindromes, 153
    refactoring, 53, 132, 165, 177–184
columns, 38
combining booleans, 40–43
command lines, DOM manipulation at,
    224–233
commands
    bundle, 238
    chmod, 23
    console.log, 18
    node, 22, 23, 83
    npm, 154, 156
    which, 18, 22

comments, 28–29. *See also* words
 documentation, 106
 JavaScript, 244
comparing numbers, 93
compatibility, browsers, 5
concatenation, 27–32
configuring
 Jekyll, 237
 JSON (JavaScript Object Notation),
   157
 repositories, 11
 testing, 154–159
`console.log`, 18, 33, 233
consoles
 browsers, 14–19, 99
 JavaScript, 18
constants, 66
constructor functions, 135
control, versions, 156
control flow, strings, 35–44
conventions
 dates, 71
 numbers, 158
 regular expressions (regexes/regexps), 74
converting numbers to strings, 67–69
copying
 files, 236
 shell scripts, 232
counting words, 86, 87
creating. *See* configuring; formatting
CSS (cascading style sheet), 229
 `current` class, 250, 251
 image gallery, 243
curly braces ({}), 32, 37
current, setting images as, 250–252
customizing days of the week, 72

D
dates, 69–73
days of the week
 customizing, 72 (*see also* dates)
 factoring in (functions), 96
debugging
 JavaScript, 99
 printing, 33

 tools, 16
default behaviors, 209
defining
 functions, 91–95, 96
 objects, 3, 135–138
 prototypes, 143
 `TranslatedPhrase` objects, 141
deploying applications, 10–13
`describe` function, 159, 160, 169
detecting palindromes, 136, 138, 154, 155,
   187–191, 216
developer tools. *See also* tools
 browsers, 17
 MDN (Mozilla Developer Network), 139,
   147, 148
documentation
 comments, 106
 for File System, 216
 JSDOM, 228
 `urllib`, 220
Document Object Model. *See* DOM
   (Document Object Model)
`document` objects, 227
documents, 196
DOM (Document Object Model), 187, 197,
   198, 215, 250
 finding elements, 253
 loading, 198, 199
 manipulation, 4
 manipulation at command lines, 224–233
dot loads, 106
dot notation, 17
double quotes ("), 25
DRY principle, 142
duplicating code
 DRY principle, 142
 eliminating, 146–147
dynamic HTML (Hypertext Markup
   Language), 202–205, 207. *See also* HTML
   (Hypertext Markup Language)

E
ECMAScript, 5, 31. *See also* JavaScript
editing GitHub Pages, 12
Eich, Brendan, 5

emojis, 108, 109
empty strings, 26
encapsulation, 96
entering long strings, 211, 212
equality, asserting, 168
equivalence classes, 124
errors
    messages, 100, 101, 170
    syntax, 27
    testing, 165
evaluation, short-circuit, 182
events, 4
    DOM (Document Object Model), 197, 198
    listeners, 187, 192–201
exec method, 76
executable scripts, 22
exponentiation, 66
exporting
    modules, 158
    Phase objects, 158
expressions, regular. *See* regular expressions

F
factoring palindrome testers into functions,
    195
fat arrow, 94–95
files
    copying, 236
    creating, 21
    functions in, 95–104
    JavaScript in, 21–22
    reading from, 216–218
    standalone JavaScript, 6
    testing, 160 (*see also* testing)
File System, documentation for, 216
filter method, 116, 122–125, 180
floating-point numbers, 65
floats. *See* floating-point numbers
forEach loops, 110–114, 116, 126, 178, 179
fork capability (GitHub Pages), 235, 237
for loops, 53, 58, 62
formatting. *See also* configuring
    code, 38–39
    files, 21
    indenting, 98

lists of images, 243
    printing, 33–35
    quotes, 26
    repositories, 11
forms. *See also* documents
    adding, 201, 207, 208
    HTML (Hypertext Markup Language), 4,
        200, 205–214
    submitting, 209
front-end JavaScript programs, 6
functionality, non-standard, 150
functional programming, 3, 95, 115–116,
    179, 180
    filter method, 122–125
    map method, 116–122
    reduce method, 126–133
    TDD (test-driven development),
        132–133
functions, 3. *See also* methods; objects
    anonymous, 110, 118, 196
    arguments, 92, 93
    auxiliary, 120, 121
    calls, 9
    console.log, 33
    constructor, 135
    defining, 91–95, 96
    describe, 159, 160, 169
    factoring palindrome testers into, 195
    fat arrow, 94–95
    in files, 95–104
    forEach loops, 110–114
    it, 159
    method chaining, 104–110
    nameless, 110
    new, 69, 75, 77
    palindrome, 104, 107, 132, 137, 140,
        141, 142
    Phrase, 135, 136, 137, 140, 142
    prompt, 190, 205
    querySelector, 229
    return values, 92
    sorting numerical arrays, 92–94
    sum, 126
    trigonometric, 66
    urlify, 120

G

general-purpose programming languages, 1
getDay() method, 95
GitHub Pages, 11, 191
   editing, 12
   fork capability, 235
   renaming, 238
   saving settings, 14
   usernames, 12
Google Translate, 226, 232
Green, testing, 172–177

H

handling HTML forms, 205–214
Hansson, David Heinemeier, 148, 149
hash symbol (#), 195
hello, world!, 6, 8, 9–10
   adding proof of concept, 187, 188
   live on web pages, 15
HTML (Hypertext Markup Language)
   adding forms, 201
   button tag, 192, 193, 206
   dynamic, 202–205, 207
   forms, 4, 200, 205–214
   image gallery (sample application), 242–243
   methods unrelated to, 47
   skeletons, 7, 8

I

identifiers, 29
image gallery (sample application), 235
   changing image info, 252–259
   deploying, 256–259
   fork capability (GitHub Pages), 235, 237
   HTML (Hypertext Markup Language), 242–243
   modifying images, 242–249
   prepping, 235–242
   setting images as current, 250–252
images
   modifying, 242–249
   updating, 254
img tags, 243
includes method, 48, 60

increment statements, 51
indenting, 98. *See also* formatting
   code, 38
indexes, 51
inheritance, 142
initializing NPM (Node Package Manager)
   modules, 157
inserting comments, 28–29. *See also* adding
Inspect Element, activating tools via, 16
installing
   Jekyll, 237
   Mocha, 154
   NPM (Node Package Manager), 219
instances
   methods, 57
   strings, 44
instantiating objects, 135
integers, summing, 127, 128
interpolation, 27–32
   backtick syntax, 31–32
inverting booleans, 40–43
iteration
   arrays, 62–64, 111, 112
   forEach loops, 110–114
   strings, 50–53, 112, 113
it function, 159

J

JavaScript
   applications, 10–13 (*see also* applications)
   in browsers, 7–14
   comments, 244
   consoles, 18
   debugging, 99
   in files, 21–22
   objects, 17 (*see also* objects)
   overview of, 5–7
   prepping, 239–240
   in REPLs (Read-Evaluate-Print Loops), 14–20
   in shell scripts, 22–23
   submitting forms, 209
JavaScript Object Notation. *See* JSON (JavaScript Object Notation)

Jekyll static site builder
  configuring, 237
  installing, 237
joining, 27. *See also* concatenation
  undoing splits, 61–62
jQuery library, 195
JSDOM
  adding, 227 (*see also* DOM [Document
    Object Model])
  documentation, 228
JSON (JavaScript Object Notation), 157

K
keys, 81
key–value pairs, 81
keywords, return, 119
Knuth, Donald, 57

L
length property, 35, 36, 52
lengths object, 129
letters method, 168, 169, 173, 174, 178,
    180, 181
listeners, events, 187, 192–201. *See also* events
lists of images, 243
literals, templates, 31–32
LiveScript. *See* JavaScript
loading
  DOMs (Document Object Models),
    198, 199
  modules, 190
logarithms, 66
long strings, entering, 211, 212
loops
  for, 53, 58, 62
  alternatives to, 116
  forEach, 110–114, 116, 126, 178, 179
  indexes, 51
  iteration, 50
  REPLs (Read-Evaluate-Print Loops), 6
lowercase letters, 46

M
main branch, serving websites from, 13
main gallery images, setting, 245
map method, 116–122

Map object, 87–89
matchers, regex, 172
match method, 78, 85
mathematics
  floating-point numbers, 65
  mathematical operations, 65–66
  + operators, 27
Math object, 66–67
  converting numbers to strings, 67–69
MDN (Mozilla Developer Network), 3, 139,
    147, 148
messages, error, 100, 101, 170
methods, 18, 91
  arrays, 59–62
  chaining, 104–110, 180
  charAt, 52, 53, 173
  exec, 76
  filter, 116, 122–125, 180
  getDay( ), 95
  includes, 48, 60
  instances, 57
  letters, 168, 169, 173, 174, 178, 180, 181
  map, 116–122
  match, 78, 85
  overriding, 143–144
  palindrome, 175
  palindromeTester, 209
  querySelector, 195
  querySelectorAll, 244
  reduce, 116, 126–133
  regular expressions (regexes/regexps), 75–76
  remove, 231
  reverse, 108, 109, 137, 150
  slice, 59
  split, 55, 79
  strings, 44–50
  toLowerCase, 107
  toString( ), 67
  unrelated to HTML, 47
mixed-cased palindromes, 164
Mocha testing tool
  installing, 154
  pending tests, 162–163
  settings, 154
  starting, 156

modifying
   `current` class, 250, 251
   image info, 252–259
   images, 242–249
   native objects, 147–152
modules
   exporting, 158
   installing NPM (Node Package Manager), 219
   loading, 190
   NPM (Node Package Manager), 4, 153, 157
   publishing, 184–186
modulo operator (%), 124
moving `processedContent` into methods, 140, 150
Mozilla Developer Network. *See* MDN (Mozilla Developer Network)

N
nameless functions, 110
names
   GitHub Pages, 12, 238
   repositories, 236
   variables, 29, 30 (*see also* identifiers)
native assertions, applying, 169
native objects, 65. *See also* objects
   dates, 69–73
   `Map` object, 87–89
   mathematical operations, 65–66
   `Math` object, 66–67
   modifying, 147–152
   numbers, 65–66
   plain objects, 81–82
   regular expressions, 73–81
   unique words, 83–89
Netscape Navigator, 5
networks, MDN. *See* MDN (Mozilla Developer Network)
`new` function, 69, 75, 77
`node` command, 22, 23, 83
Node.js, 18–20
   shell scripts, 215 (*see also* shell scripts)
Node package Manager. *See* NPM (Node Package Manager)
Node REPL, 23, 38, 69, 83, 106. *See also* REPLs (Read-Evaluate-Print Loops)

non-standard functionality, 150
notation, 244
   bracket ([]), 56
   JSON (JavaScript Object Notation), 157
notifications, adding, 203
NPM (Node Package Manager), 4, 6
   `browserify` utility, 188, 189, 191
   installing, 219
   modules, 153, 157
   publishing, 184–186
`npm` command, 154, 156
`null` objects, 197
numbers, 65–66
   comparing, 93
   conventions, 158
   converting strings, 67–69
   dates, 69–73
   floating-point, 65
numerical arrays, sorting, 92–94

O
object-oriented languages, 17, 44
objects
   built-in, 3
   defining, 3, 135–138
   `document`, 227
   functions attached to, 91 (*see also* functions; methods)
   instantiating, 135
   JavaScript, 17
   JSON (JavaScript Object Notation), 157
   `lengths`, 129
   `Map`, 87–89
   modifying native, 147–152
   native, 65 (*see also* native objects)
   `null`, 197
   plain, 81–82
   prototypes, 30
operators
   +, 27
   !, 42, 43
   &&, 40, 41
   ||, 41
   modulo operator (%), 124
overriding methods, 143–144

P

palindrome function, 104, 107, 132, 137, 140, 141, 142, 175

palindromes
- adding forms, 207, 208
- adding HTML for results, 202
- code, 153
- creating pages, 187–191
- detecting, 136, 138, 154, 155, 187–191, 216
- factoring testers into functions, 195
- long strings, 212
- mixed-cased, 164
- punctuated, 167
- testing, 160, 166
- translating, 144

palindromeTester method, 209

paragraphs
- pulling out, 230
- shell scripts, 231

passwords, 40

pasting shell scripts, 232

pending tests, 162–163

Perl, 215

Phrase function, 135, 136, 137, 140, 142

phrases, 3

piping, 232

plain objects, 81–82

popping arrays, 61

powers, 66

prepping
- image gallery (sample application), 235–242
- JavaScript, 239–240

printing strings, 33–35

processedContent, moving into methods, 140, 150

programming languages
- functional programming, 95
- general-purpose, 1
- HTML (Hypertext Markup Language), 4 (see also HTML [Hypertext Markup Language])
- object-oriented languages, 17

programs. See also applications
- front-end JavaScript, 6

hello, world!, 6, 8, 9–10 (see also hello, world!)

image gallery (see image gallery [sample application])

wikp, 224

writing, 6

prompt function, 190, 205

prompts, 4
- Node.js, 18–20

properties, 82
- assigning, 135
- length, 35, 36, 52
- strings, 35–44

prototype-based languages, 139

prototypes, 139–147
- chains, 139
- defining, 143
- objects, 30, 139 (see also objects)

publishing NPM (Node Package Manager) modules, 184–186

punctuated palindromes, testing, 167

pushing, 179
- arrays, 61
- characters, 173

Python, 215

Q

querySelectorAll method, 244

querySelector method, 195, 229

R

Rails, 205

Read-Evaluate-Print Loops. See REPLs (Read-Evaluate-Print Loops)

reading
- from files, 216–218
- from URLs, 218–223

Real Programming, 21

Red, testing, 164–172

reduce method, 116, 126–133

refactoring code, 53, 132, 165, 177–184

references
- regular expressions, 75
- viewing, 230

regex matchers, 172. See also regular expressions

regressions, 165

regular expressions (regexes/regexps), 56,
    73–81
    methods, 75–76
    online builders, 74
    references, 75
    string methods, 77–80
reloading
    pages, 101
    palindrome function, 107
remove method, 231
renaming
    GitHub Pages, 238
    repositories, 236
repeating, DRY principle, 142
REPLs (Read-Evaluate-Print Loops), 6, 100.
        See also Node REPL
    applying calculators, 66
    code in, 39
    JavaScript in, 14–20
    loading files into, 138
    quotes and, 26
    shell scripts, 217 (*see also* shell scripts)
    strings and, 25
repositories
    creating, 11
    image gallery, 235, 236 (*see also* image gallery
        [sample application])
resources, MDN (Mozilla Developer Network),
    3
result areas, 204
return keyword, 119
return values, 92
reverse method, 108, 109, 137, 150
reversing
    arrays, 60
    strings, 106
roots, 66
Ruby, 215

S

sample applications. *See* image gallery (sample
    application)
saving GitHub settings, 14
scope, variables, 63
scripting languages, 22, 215

scripts
    executable, 22
    shell, 4, 6 (*see also* shell scripts)
script tags, 9
semantic versioning, 158
sequences, string literals, 25. *see also* strings
settings. *See also* configuring; formatting
    editing GitHub Pages, 12
    Mocha, 154
    saving (GitHub), 14
shell scripts, 4, 6, 215
    Bash (Bourne-again shell), 6
    copying, 232
    DOM manipulation at command lines,
        224–233
    JavaScript in, 22–23
    paragraphs, 231
    pasting, 232
    reading from files, 216–218
    reading from URLs, 218–223
short-circuit evaluation, 182
Sinatra, 205
single quote ('), 25
slash (/) character, 28–29
slice method, 59
slicing arrays, 58–59
sorting
    arrays, 60
    numerical arrays, 92–94
split method, 79
splitting
    arrays, 55–56
    undoing splits, 61–62
src attribute, 100
standalone JavaScript files, 6
starting
    image gallery (sample application), 235–242
    Mocha, 156
state/length correspondence, troubleshooting,
    130, 131
statements
    console.log, 233
    increment, 51
strict equality, asserting, 168
strings

backtick syntax, 31–32
booleans, 35–44
concatenation, 27–32
control flow, 35–44
creating URL-appropriate for arrays, 118
empty, 26
entering, 211, 212
`filter` method, 122–125
instances, 44
interpolation, 27–32
iteration, 50–53, 112, 113
literals, 25, 30
methods, 44–50
+ operators, 27
overview of, 25–27
printing, 33–35
properties, 35–44
regular expressions (regexes/regexps), 77–80
reversing, 106
stubs, adding, 169
submitting forms, 209
`sum` function, 126
summing integers, 127, 128
synchronous versions, 216
syntax
    backtick, 31–32
    defining functions, 96
    errors, 27

T

tables, truth, 40, 41
tags. *See also* HTML (Hypertext Markup
    Language)
`button`, 192, 193, 206
`img`, 243
`script`, 9
TDD (test-driven development), 3, 53, 153. *See
    also* testing
    functional programming, *132–133*
    when to use, 165
technical sophistication, 1, 47
    applying, 28
    definition of, 2–3
templates, literals, 31–32
test-driven development. *See* TDD (test-driven
    development)

testing, 153
    adding, 169
    breaking, 164
    configuring, 154–159
    errors, 165
    Green, 172–177
    initial coverage, 159–164
    Mocha (*see* Mocha)
    palindromes, 160, 166
    pending tests, 162–163
    publishing NPMs (Node Package Managers),
        184–186
    Red, 164–172
    refactoring code, 177–184
    when to test, 165
tests
    automated, 132
    suites, 160, 161, 167 (*see also* testing)
    suites, running, 179
text-to-speech. *See* TTS (text-to-speech)
thumbnails, 249. *See also* images
titles, updating images, 254
`toLowerCase` method, 107
tools
    activating, 16
    browser consoles, 14–19
    browser developer, 17
    `browserify` utility, 188, 189, 191
    debugging, 16
    Mocha, 154 (*see also* testing)
`toString()` method, 67
`TranslatedPhrase` objects, 141, 142
translating palindromes, 144
trigonometric functions, 66
triple equals, 36
troubleshooting
    bugfixes, 157
    filtering, 123, 125
    state/length correspondence, 130, 131
truth tables, 40, 41
TTS (text-to-speech), 224

U

undoing splits, 61–62
unique words, 83–89

updating
    `alt` attributes, 247
    images, 254
uppercase letters, 46
`urlify` function, 120
`urllib` documentation, 220
URLs (Uniform Resource Locators), reading
    from, 218–223
usernames, GitHub Pages, 12. *See also* names

V
values
    boolean, 36 (*see also* booleans)
    key–value pairs, 81
Vanier, Mike, 64, 121, 122
variables, 29
    assigning, 29, 31
    creating, 110, 111
    interpolation, 27–32
    names, 29, 30
    scope, 63
    string concatenation and, 29 (*see also*
        concatenation)
versions, 5
    control, 156
    semantic versioning, 158
    synchronous, 216

viewing
    JavaScript, 7–14
    references, 230

W
web applications, testing, 153. *See also*
    applications
web inspectors, 230
web pages, viewing JavaScript in, 7–14
`which` command, 18, 22
`wikp` program, 224
wild buttons, 194
words
    counting, 86, 87
    unique, 83–89
writing
    comments, 28–29
    to console logs, 34
    programs, 6
    shell scripts, 215 (*see also*
        shell scripts)

Z
zeros, 157
Zip codes, 75, 76, 77

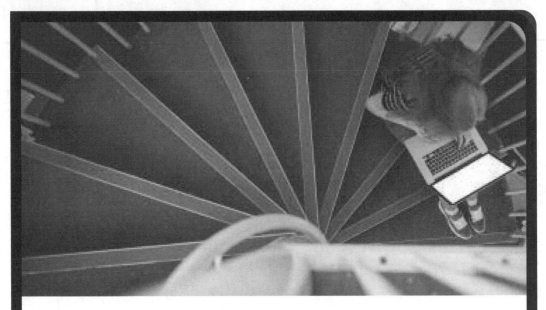

Photo by Marvent/Shutterstock

VIDEO TRAINING FOR THE **IT PROFESSIONAL**

LEARN QUICKLY
Learn a new technology in just hours. Video training can teach more in less time, and material is generally easier to absorb and remember.

WATCH AND LEARN
Instructors demonstrate concepts so you see technology in action.

TEST YOURSELF
Our Complete Video Courses offer self-assessment quizzes throughout.

CONVENIENT
Most videos are streaming with an option to download lessons for offline viewing.

Learn more, browse our store, and watch free, sample lessons at
informit.com/video

Save 50%* off the list price of video courses with discount code **VIDBOB**

Photo by izusek/gettyima

Register Your Product at informit.com/register

Access additional benefits and **save 35%** on your next purchase

- Automatically receive a coupon for 35% off your next purchase, valid for 30 days. Look for your code in your InformIT cart or the Manage Codes section of your account page.

- Download available product updates.

- Access bonus material if available.*

- Check the box to hear from us and receive exclusive offers on new editions and related products.

Registration benefits vary by product. Benefits will be listed on your account page under Registered Products.

InformIT.com—The Trusted Technology Learning Source

InformIT is the online home of information technology brands at Pearson, the world's foremost education company. At InformIT.com, you can:

- Shop our books, eBooks, software, and video training
- Take advantage of our special offers and promotions (informit.com/promotions)
- Sign up for special offers and content newsletter (informit.com/newsletters)
- Access thousands of free chapters and video lessons

Connect with InformIT—Visit informit.com/community

Addison-Wesley • Adobe Press • Cisco Press • Microsoft Press • Pearson IT Certification • Que • Sams • Peachpit Press

 Pearson